Ethics and Intelligence

AURORA AMORIS

ETHICS AND INTELLIGENCE

Questions of Morality in the Age of AI

2025

Ethics and Intelligence

Aurora Amoris

CONTENTS

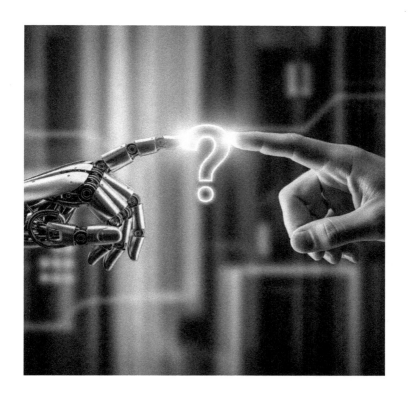

CHAPTER 1

Artificial Intelligence and Ethics: Basic Questions

1.1. Artificial Intelligence and Human Rights

Artificial intelligence (AI) has grow to be an integral a part of cutting-edge society, influencing numerous factors of lifestyles. As its presence continues to increase, it's miles important to evaluate the capacity impact of AI on human rights.

One of the primary worries regarding AI and human rights is the problem of privacy. AI structures often require sizeable quantities of personal information to function efficaciously, which can raise widespread privateness worries. These structures can collect, save, and manner sensitive data approximately individuals, such as fitness records, monetary facts, and private possibilities. If mishandled, this information may be exploited, main to breaches of privacy and the violation of an person's right to control their private data.

The growing reliance on AI for duties which includes surveillance and predictive analytics in addition complicates the problem of privacy. AI technology enable mass information series and real-time monitoring of people, doubtlessly infringing on their rights to privateness and freedom from unwarranted surveillance. In a few cases, using AI for surveillance may even lead to authorities overreach and authoritarian practices, threatening non-public freedoms.

As AI structures end up greater advanced, ensuring records protection becomes important. Strong regulatory frameworks are had to shield individuals' privacy rights and establish clear suggestions on how personal records ought to be treated, processed, and shared. The ethical use of AI have to prioritize human rights, especially the right to privacy, a good way to save you misuse.

AI has the capacity to reinforce present social biases and perpetuate discrimination. Machine gaining knowledge of algorithms often rely upon historical records to make selections, and if that statistics is biased, the AI device may also reflect the ones biases in its outcomes. This is specially concerning while AI is utilized in areas inclusive of hiring, law enforcement, and lending, wherein biased selections could have significant effects for individuals.

For example, AI structures utilized in recruitment strategies may additionally prefer certain demographic organizations over others, based totally on biased statistics that reflects historical inequalities. Similarly, predictive policing algorithms can disproportionately goal marginalized communities, reinforcing systemic racism and discrimination.

Addressing AI bias is important in making sure that human rights, specially the right to equality and non-discrimination, are upheld. It is important to broaden AI systems which are obvious and accountable, with mechanisms in location to detect and accurate biased algorithms.

Additionally, making sure diversity in the groups that create AI technology can help mitigate bias and make sure that those structures are honest and just.

Another widespread human rights problem related to AI is the virtual divide—the space between those who have get admission to to advanced technologies and people who do no longer. While AI has the potential to force development and improve great of lifestyles, its blessings may not be similarly distributed. People in underserved communities or developing countries might also lack the assets or infrastructure to access AI technology, exacerbating current inequalities.

This disparity in get right of entry to to AI technologies can cause in addition marginalization of prone populations, denying them the opportunities to advantage from improvements in healthcare, training, and employment. In the context of human rights, the right to get admission to technology and the digital international is increasingly more visible as crucial. Efforts have to be made to bridge the digital divide by using making sure that AI is available to all, no matter geographic place or socio-financial repute.

The upward thrust of AI and automation also poses demanding situations to hard work rights, particularly the capability displacement of people. AI systems and robots are more and more getting used to perform responsibilities historically achieved by means of people, main to issues approximately activity loss and economic inequality. In sectors inclusive of production, transportation, and customer support, AI has the ability to replace human people, leaving many individuals without employment possibilities.

From a human rights angle, the right to work is fundamental. It is crucial to address the capability bad influences of AI on employment via developing policies that defend workers' rights inside the face of automation. These policies might also include retraining programs, social safety nets, and projects to make sure that AI technology are used to complement in preference to replace human labor.

AI affords both possibilities and demanding situations when it comes to human rights. On one hand, it has the capability to improve exceptional of existence, enhance get admission to to services, and make contributions to social progress. On the opposite hand, if not properly managed, AI can exacerbate privateness violations, support discrimination, and create monetary inequalities. To make certain that AI respects and protects human rights, it's far essential to set up sturdy ethical pointers, regulatory frameworks, and oversight mechanisms. As AI maintains to conform, it is crucial to prioritize human rights in its development and deployment to create a honest and simply society for all.

1.2. Moral Issues of AI

The development and integration of artificial intelligence (AI) into numerous sectors of society increases profound ethical troubles that call for cautious exam. AI is transforming the panorama of era, however it additionally brings with it complicated questions on obligation, ethics, and the future of humanity. The ethical demanding situations posed through AI pass past the competencies of the technology itself; they involve how AI structures are designed, applied, and applied in society.

One of the most urgent ethical issues related to AI is accountability. As AI systems turn out to be greater self sufficient and capable of making decisions, it will become more and more difficult to pinpoint who's accountable while those structures make mistakes or reason harm. For example, in the context of self-riding motors, if an twist of fate occurs, it is doubtful whether or not the duty lies with the producer, the software developers, or the folks that own and perform the car.

This ambiguity approximately responsibility increases fundamental moral questions. If an AI device makes a decision that leads to damage, how ought to liability be determined? Can a device be held morally accountable for its movements, or is the blame constantly attributed to its creators or operators? These questions task traditional notions of responsibility, which are typically based totally on human agency and aim. As AI structures become extra independent, the need for brand new prison frameworks and ethical tips to address those issues will become vital.

AI has the potential to result in sizable benefits, however it additionally poses risks, mainly while it's miles used in approaches that aren't well regulated or controlled. The ability for AI to reason damage is particularly regarding in regions consisting of healthcare, crook justice, and warfare. For instance, AI-powered algorithms used in predictive policing or sentencing ought to toughen present biases and cause discriminatory practices, even as AI used in army drones could be used to carry out self sustaining strikes with little human oversight.

The possibility that AI may be used maliciously, along with within the advent of deepfakes or in cyberattacks, also increases ethical worries. These programs of AI will be used to manipulate people, unfold misinformation, and destabilize societies. In the wrong palms, AI might be weaponized, main to considerable damage. Thus, one of the number one ethical worries surrounding AI is making sure that it's far used responsibly and that appropriate safeguards are installed area to prevent its misuse.

Another widespread ethical issue surrounding AI is the query of autonomy. As AI structures end up more able to making selections without direct human intervention, they're more and more visible as self reliant dealers. This raises questions on the character of AI selection-making and whether or not machines can truely make moral alternatives. Can a system be trusted to make morally sound selections, or is the idea of ethical company something this is inherently human?

In a few cases, AI structures may be programmed to follow ethical ideas, along with the Asimov-stimulated "Three Laws of Robotics." However, those regulations are far from best and can fail to account for the complexities of real-global conditions. Furthermore, AI structures can handiest operate in the parameters set with the aid of their creators, because of this that they may replicate the biases, prejudices, and ethical shortcomings of the individuals who layout them.

The issue of AI autonomy additionally increases concerns approximately the position of human oversight. Should AI structures be allowed to make decisions completely on their personal, or need to humans always keep the final say? There is a delicate stability between empowering AI to make decisions and preserving human control to make certain that these selections align with ethical and moral values.

One of the most debatable packages of AI is in navy and defense technology. The use of AI in self sustaining guns structures, which includes drones and robots, increases giant ethical and moral questions about the function of machines in conflict. The capability for AI to make lifestyles-or-demise decisions without human intervention has sparked debates about the morality of delegating such vital choices to machines.

Proponents of AI in warfare argue that AI structures may be more particular and powerful than human beings, potentially reducing civilian casualties and improving the performance of military operations. However, critics contend that the usage of self sustaining guns structures may want to cause uncontrollable escalation, with machines making decisions based on algorithms instead of human judgment. There is also issue that AI-powered guns may be used by oppressive regimes to carry out unjust wars or suppress dissent.

The ethical dilemma of AI in battle lies in the question of whether it is morally ideal to allow machines to take lifestyles-or-loss of life selections. Can machines apprehend the complexities of warfare and the cost of human lifestyles, or are they definitely executing programmed instructions? The ethical implications of AI in war are extensive and want to be carefully taken into consideration as these technology retain to increase.

As AI structures end up extra incorporated into various sectors, there's a developing situation about the ability dehumanization of work. Machines are increasingly more capable of appearing tasks that were once accomplished with the aid of people, from manual hard work to complicated decision-making. This raises the query of the way AI's growing function in the personnel would possibly affect human dignity and the cost of human hard work.

The ethical implications of AI within the team of workers go past worries about job displacement. There is a danger that AI could contribute to a society in which human people are seen as expendable, and their roles are reduced to responsibilities which are repetitive or menial. In such a situation, the human detail of labor might be faded, and individuals can be left with little sense of reason or fulfillment of their jobs.

Furthermore, AI systems utilized in hiring, performance critiques, and other factors of human resources should make a contribution to new sorts of discrimination, reinforcing existing social inequalities. The ethical assignment lies in ensuring that AI is used in ways that decorate human dignity and nicely-being, in preference to diminishing it.

In healthcare, AI offers the capacity for advanced diagnostics, personalized remedy plans, and extra efficient healthcare structures. However, the usage of AI in this discipline additionally raises vital ethical troubles. For example, AI systems used for medical choice-making should be designed to prioritize affected person welfare and respect people' rights. There is a danger that AI can be used to make choices that prioritize price-effectiveness over affected person care, leading to situations wherein people are dealt with as facts factors as opposed to people.

Another ethical difficulty in healthcare is the issue of informed consent. As AI systems turn out to be more involved in scientific diagnoses and remedies, sufferers have to be completely informed about the role AI plays in their care. They need to have the right to pick whether or not or not they want to be treated by AI-pushed systems and have to be confident that these structures are obvious, reliable, and responsible.

The ethical troubles surrounding AI are complicated and multifaceted, ranging from questions of responsibility and obligation to issues approximately autonomy, privateness, and the capability for damage. As AI continues to conform, it is essential that those troubles be addressed via thoughtful ethical frameworks and regulatory measures. The purpose must be to make sure that AI is advanced and used in ways that align with human values and promote the nicely-being of society. The moral challenges posed with the aid of AI are not just technical in nature; they're basically approximately how we, as a society, pick out to define and uphold ethical standards within the face of unexpectedly advancing technology.

1.3. The Evolution of Ethical Thought

Ethical notion has developed notably all through records, formed by philosophical, cultural, and technological developments. As humanity advances, so too does our know-how of morality, as we confront new challenges and dilemmas delivered on by way of modifications in society, technology, and our surroundings.

The origins of moral idea can be traced again to historical civilizations, in which philosophers started out to contemplate questions of proper and incorrect, justice, and distinctive feature. In Ancient Greece, thinkers like Socrates, Plato, and Aristotle laid the groundwork for Western moral philosophy. Socrates' emphasis on self-exam and the pursuit of moral virtue thru expertise influenced generations of thinkers. Plato's idealism presented a vision of an ordered, rational universe, wherein ethical moves aligned with the pursuit of truth and justice. Aristotle, then again, developed a more sensible method to ethics, focusing on the idea of distinctive feature ethics. According to Aristotle, residing a ethical existence became approximately cultivating virtuous behavior that led to the development of right person.

In the East, ancient ethical systems together with Confucianism, Buddhism, and Hinduism additionally explored moral standards, specializing in concord, compassion, and the pursuit of spiritual enlightenment. Confucian ethics, for instance, emphasized the significance of relationships, respect for authority, and social harmony, at the same time as Buddhism promoted the reduction of suffering and the cultivation of compassion via mindfulness and meditation.

During the medieval length, ethical idea have become closely motivated with the aid of spiritual doctrine, particularly in the Abrahamic faiths. In Christianity, Judaism, and Islam, ethical standards were grounded in divine commandments and the will of God. Philosophers like St. Augustine and Thomas Aquinas included classical philosophy with non secular teachings to shape systems of ethics that had been now not simplest worried with human moves but additionally with the closing aim of salvation and the afterlife.

Medieval moral thought frequently revolved around questions of morality inside the context of spiritual responsibilities, justice, and sin. In this era, the idea of natural regulation become developed, which held that moral standards may be derived from human nature and the world round us, as created by using God. The perception of divine command idea, which posited that ethical movements have been those who aligned with God's will, dominated a good deal of the ethical discourse for the duration of this time.

The Enlightenment marked a pivotal shift in ethical thought, as the focus moved from divine commandments to human motive and individual autonomy. Thinkers like Immanuel Kant, John Locke, and Jean-Jacques Rousseau puzzled traditional authority and the function of faith in shaping moral structures. Kant's deontological ethics, as an instance, emphasised the importance of responsibility and ethical regulation, affirming that people should act consistent with typical standards that might be rationally willed via all rational beings. For Kant, morality was now not approximately the effects of actions however approximately the intentions at the back of them, guided by using purpose and the explicit imperative.

John Locke's social contract concept motivated present day political ethics, emphasizing the significance of person rights and the position of presidency in protective these rights. Rousseau's ideas about democracy and equality highlighted the moral importance of collective choice-making and the not unusual correct.

The Enlightenment also saw the upward push of utilitarianism, championed via figures like Jeremy Bentham and John Stuart Mill. Utilitarianism posited that the right action become the one that produced the greatest happiness for the greatest variety of people. This consequentialist idea shifted the focal point of ethical choice-making from responsibilities or ethical laws to the consequences of moves, leading to a greater sensible approach to ethics that would be carried out to social and political issues.

In the cutting-edge generation, moral thought persevered to diversify, motivated with the aid of developments in technology, era, and philosophy. The introduction of industrialization and globalization delivered new moral demanding situations, which includes problems of social justice, human rights, and economic inequality. The rise of existentialism, led by philosophers like Jean-Paul Sartre and Simone de Beauvoir, emphasised character freedom, responsibility, and the search for meaning in an frequently detached universe. Existentialist ethics rejected frequent moral laws and as a substitute targeted on the significance of personal choice and authenticity.

The 20th century also noticed the development of ethical relativism, which rejected the concept of absolute moral truths and rather argued that moral values and norms had been shaped by using cultural, historic, and social contexts. This view challenged the universality of ethical concepts, suggesting that ethical judgments had been subjective and dependent on character or societal perspectives.

Postmodernism in addition complex ethical thought by means of thinking the very foundations of understanding and morality. Postmodern philosophers like Michel Foucault and Jacques Derrida critiqued the grand narratives of traditional ethics, suggesting that ethical systems were merchandise of electricity relations and social constructs. Postmodernism rejected the idea of objective, time-honored truths and rather targeted at the fluidity and contingency of ethical values.

As we entered the 21st century, the fast development of generation, especially in fields like synthetic intelligence, biotechnology, and genetic engineering, added new ethical challenges that could not be absolutely addressed through conventional moral frameworks. The upward thrust of AI, particularly, raises questions on the character of machine awareness, the morality of self reliant choice-making, and the moral implications of making sensible structures which can surpass human competencies.

Ethical thinkers are grappling with the consequences of AI inside the context of current ethical frameworks. For example, the idea of gadget ethics — the question of whether AI may be programmed to act ethically — has won widespread interest. The development of self sustaining structures that make choices with out human intervention challenges our knowledge of duty, duty, and moral enterprise. Questions together with whether or not AI need to be granted legal rights, or how it can be held accountable for its actions, are primary to present day moral debates.

Furthermore, the rapid pace of technological trade has raised concerns about the erosion of privacy, the consequences of surveillance technology, and the potential for AI to exacerbate social inequalities. The moral challenges posed by way of AI require new procedures to moral reasoning that keep in mind the complexities and uncertainties of rising technologies.

The speedy upward thrust of AI calls for the variation of moral theories to address the new realities of an an increasing number of computerized world. Deontological ethics, utilitarianism, and distinctive feature ethics all provide capacity frameworks for knowledge AI's ethical implications, but every faces demanding situations whilst carried out to gadget decision-making. For instance, deontologists may struggle with how to follow categorical imperatives to self sufficient machines, even as utilitarians ought to confront the difficulty of calculating the outcomes of AI moves in complex and dynamic structures.

Virtue ethics, which emphasizes the development of desirable individual and ethical knowledge, may provide a more bendy method to AI ethics. By focusing on the virtues that AI systems should encompass — such as fairness, transparency, and empathy — distinctive feature ethics ought to assist manual the development of AI technology that align with human values.

The evolution of moral idea displays humanity's ongoing attempt to recognize and navigate the complexities of morality, particularly as new technologies emerge. From the historical cognizance on distinctive feature and justice to the modern emphasis on rights, autonomy, and effects, ethical systems have tailored to fulfill the demanding situations of their time. As AI and different superior technology keep to form our global, it's far vital that moral frameworks evolve to deal with the precise moral dilemmas they gift. The destiny of ethics in the age of AI will probable contain a synthesis of conventional moral principles with new approaches that recollect the capabilities and dangers of emerging technology.

1.4. Ethical Frameworks for AI Development

The ascent of artificial intelligence has delivered one of the maximum transformative technological forces in human records. Its growing presence across critical domain names— ranging from healthcare and training to conflict and finance— has no longer best redefined human capabilities but also rekindled foundational questions on moral duty, employer, and justice. As AI systems start to make selections formerly reserved for human judgment, the call for for certainly articulated ethical frameworks turns into greater pressing and complicated. These frameworks are not merely theoretical physical games; they form the moral scaffolding upon which societies ought to anchor the deployment and governance of smart machines. Without them, the advancement of AI can also outpace our capability to manipulate its results, risking damage to people, communities, or even future generations.

The development of ethical frameworks for AI starts offevolved with the popularity that shrewd systems do now not function in isolation. They are designed, trained, and deployed by human actors embedded in tricky social, political, and monetary systems. These human choices—what data to accumulate, what targets to optimize, what behaviors to praise—are deeply fee-laden. Ethical AI improvement, consequently, calls for a essential reflection at the assumptions embedded in code and a planned effort to align technological abilities with shared human values. This alignment, but, is not any smooth challenge. Societies round the arena vary of their ethical traditions, cultural norms, and political priorities. The mission of constructing ethical AI frameworks should, consequently, balance universality with cultural particularity, technical rigor with ethical sensitivity, and innovation with precaution.

At the heart of any moral framework lies a hard and fast of principles that manual conduct and selection-making. In the context of AI, those ideas have developed over time, inspired through each philosophical traditions and actual-international technological tendencies. One of the maximum widely usual starting points is the dedication to human dignity and autonomy. Intelligent systems need to augment in place of undermine man or woman business enterprise. This precept challenges the development of structures that manipulate user behavior, make the most cognitive biases, or render opaque the strategies by way of which choices are made. It affirms that individuals have a right to recognize, question, and decide out of algorithmic systems that have an effect on their lives in meaningful approaches. In realistic phrases, this means embedding explainability into AI layout, making sure that customers aren't simply passive recipients of machine choices but informed contributors in virtual environments.

Closely associated with autonomy is the principle of fairness. Fairness in AI is notoriously hard to define and operationalize, yet it stays significant to any moral evaluation. AI structures trained on historic statistics can reproduce and even exacerbate societal biases, main to discriminatory results in hiring, lending, policing, and past. An moral framework have to therefore deal with no longer most effective the overall performance metrics of an algorithm however the distributive justice of its results. Fairness calls for a deep interrogation of schooling facts, modeling alternatives, and deployment contexts. It needs non-stop monitoring and the willingness to remodel systems in mild of their real-international influences. Moreover, fairness isn't always a one-size-fits-all concept; it varies relying at the values of the communities affected. Thus, ethical AI improvement should contain participatory procedures that consist of diverse voices in defining what fairness method in particular contexts.

Another foundational element is duty. AI systems can obfuscate strains of duty, in particular whilst choices emerge from complicated neural networks or when multiple actors— records carriers, software program builders, device integrators—make a contribution to a given system. Ethical frameworks need to ensure that accountability is preserved at every degree of the AI lifecycle. This entails not only technical mechanisms which includes audit trails and model documentation but additionally felony and institutional mechanisms that assign duty and permit redress. Accountability also extends to broader societal harms, inclusive of the effect of automation on employment or the environmental expenses of schooling massive models. In this regard, ethical frameworks should inspire a holistic information of AI's effects, resisting the temptation to recognition narrowly on technical performance whilst ignoring systemic consequences.

Transparency is frequently championed as a cornerstone of moral AI, yet its implementation is fraught with demanding situations. Many AI models, particularly the ones based on deep getting to know, perform as black bins, rendering their selection methods unintelligible even to their creators. Ethical frameworks must grapple with the change-offs among overall performance and interpretability, pushing for advances in explainable AI while acknowledging the restrictions of cutting-edge strategies. Transparency also includes openness approximately data resources, assumptions, boundaries, and capability dangers. It isn't enough to put up technical papers or supply code; significant transparency requires speaking with affected groups in handy and sincere methods. Furthermore, transparency isn't merely a rely of disclosure but of consider-building. Ethical frameworks have to foster a way of life wherein transparency is valued not as a compliance requirement but as a ethical duty to those impacted by means of AI structures.

Privacy, long a vital subject in digital ethics, takes on new dimensions inside the age of AI. Machine learning structures depend closely on big datasets, frequently containing sensitive private statistics. Ethical frameworks need to protect person privateness now not only through technical safeguards inclusive of encryption and differential privacy but also via normative commitments to statistics minimization, informed consent, and motive issue. Moreover, privateness have to be understood in relational phrases: it is not merely about controlling statistics but approximately preserving the dignity and autonomy of individuals in datafied environments. The rise of surveillance technologies, mainly in authoritarian contexts, underscores the urgency of embedding sturdy privateness protections in AI development. At the same time, ethical frameworks should navigate tensions among privacy and other values, such as public health or safety, calling for nuanced deliberation rather than absolutist positions.

Beyond those center ideas, moral frameworks must cope with the wider social and geopolitical implications of AI. The deployment of AI technologies often reflects and reinforces present electricity structures. Wealthy companies and governments wield disproportionate influence over the improvement and use of AI, elevating issues approximately monopolization, digital colonialism, and technocratic governance. Ethical AI need to be attentive to those dynamics, advocating for inclusive governance systems, equitable access to advantages, and resistance to the concentration of strength. This consists of support for open-supply projects, investment in public-hobby AI research, and mechanisms for international cooperation. Moreover, moral frameworks should anticipate the global diffusion of AI and the want for pass-cultural speak. While widespread ideas can offer a shared foundation, their interpretation and application have to recognize cultural range and neighborhood priorities.

Institutional efforts to codify ethical standards have proliferated in recent years, reflecting the growing popularity of the want for ethical steering in AI development. Organizations together with the European Commission, the OECD, the IEEE, and UNESCO have released suggestions emphasizing human-centric values, honest layout, and sustainable innovation. These documents range in scope and enforceability, however they collectively signal a large consensus at the significance of ethics in AI. Yet critics warn of "ethics washing," wherein groups undertake ethical language to deflect criticism with out substantively converting practices. Ethical frameworks should consequently be sponsored through mechanisms of responsibility, enforcement, and public scrutiny. This includes regulatory oversight, professional codes of conduct, and civil society engagement. Ethics can not continue to be a count number of aspiration; it ought to be institutionalized in methods that shape actual-international conduct.

A specifically thorny undertaking for moral AI is the query of ethical pluralism. Different societies hold divergent perspectives on fundamental values which include freedom, equality, authority, and network. What one lifestyle deems proper—say, predictive policing or facial recognition—every other may additionally locate abhorrent. Ethical frameworks have to navigate these variations with out succumbing to relativism or imperialism. One method is to anchor ethical concepts in the world over diagnosed human rights, which offer a normative baseline while allowing for cultural variation. Another is to foster deliberative strategies that deliver collectively various stakeholders to negotiate ethical standards. Ethical AI development isn't always in reality a technical endeavor; it's miles a democratic task that must be guided by inclusive and participatory methods.

As AI systems grow greater self sufficient and integrated into selection-making, the moral stakes turn out to be even better. Questions as soon as restrained to philosophical debates now demand practical answers. Can a self-using car prioritize lives in an coincidence scenario? Should a hiring set of rules be allowed to make final decisions? How can we make certain that AI-generated content respects truth and avoids manipulation?

These dilemmas resist smooth solutions, and ethical frameworks should be flexible enough to house ongoing mirrored image and mastering. Moreover, the speedy pace of AI innovation needs a dynamic method to ethics. Frameworks ought to be updated in reaction to new competencies, emergent dangers, and transferring societal expectations. Static codes are insufficient; what is wanted are dwelling ethical infrastructures that evolve with the technology they govern.

Looking forward, moral frameworks for AI must enlarge their temporal and ecological horizons. The effect of AI isn't always limited to offer customers or instantaneous programs. Decisions made today about information collection, version layout, and device deployment will shape the future in profound methods. Ethical AI have to incorporate concepts of intergenerational justice, considering the long-term outcomes on social structures, democratic institutions, and the surroundings. In precise, the electricity needs of schooling large fashions improve questions on sustainability and climate effect. An ethical AI framework should be as worried with planetary health as with algorithmic fairness. It have to renowned that technological progress isn't inherently virtuous; its price depends on how it serves the commonplace right.

The development of moral frameworks for AI is an inherently interdisciplinary and collaborative venture. It requires the insights of ethicists, technologists, social scientists, prison scholars, policy-makers, and—crucially—the voices of those most laid low with AI structures. It demands humility, vigilance, and a willingness to confront uncomfortable truths. Ethics should no longer be reduced to a tick list or an afterthought; it need to be integrated into each level of the AI lifecycle. The future of synthetic intelligence will be fashioned not handiest by what we can construct but by means of what we select to construct. Ethical frameworks are our compass in that adventure. They remind us that technological electricity includes moral obligation and that the choices we make these days will echo a ways into the destiny. The degree of AI's success will no longer be its intelligence however its alignment with our maximum ethical aspirations.

1.5. The Challenge of Bias in AI Systems

In the coronary heart of each synthetic intelligence device lies a constellation of records, algorithms, and selection-making architectures built via human arms. These systems promise objectivity, scalability, and performance, yet satirically, they frequently inherit the imperfections, prejudices, and inequalities embedded in the societies that design them. Among the most pressing worries confronting the destiny of AI is the continual and pervasive task of bias. Bias in AI isn't an summary or theoretical flaw; it is a measurable and consequential fact with implications for justice, opportunity, and human dignity. From hiring platforms that prefer male candidates to predictive policing systems that disproportionately target minority groups, biased AI threatens to reproduce and increase the very kinds of discrimination that many was hoping shrewd machines would transcend. Understanding, figuring out, and mitigating bias in AI systems is as a consequence not merely a technical imperative but an ethical, social, and political one.

Bias, in its maximum wellknown feel, refers to systematic deviation from neutrality or equity. In the context of AI, it manifests when an algorithm constantly produces outputs that choose or drawback unique people or agencies, regularly along lines of race, gender, elegance, or geography. Importantly, this is not constantly the result of intentional prejudice at the a part of developers. More regularly, bias emerges subtly, as an unintentional outcome of design choices, facts limitations, or institutional priorities. This makes it all the extra insidious—bias in AI is rarely a count number of a single flaw but the cumulative impact of infinite decisions, each apparently rational or benign in isolation, yet discriminatory in combination.

At the inspiration of any AI device lies information. Data serves as the lifeblood of gadget gaining knowledge of, supplying the uncooked fabric from which algorithms parent patterns, generate predictions, and automate tasks. However, actual-world statistics is a long way from neutral. It displays the behaviors, decisions, and inequalities of beyond and gift societies. Historical hiring information, as an example, might also reveal longstanding gender imbalances in technical roles, not because women are much less capable, however because of many years of exclusion, bias, and social conditioning. When such data is used to train hiring algorithms, the device may additionally "study" that male applicants are most well known, no longer recognizing that this is a mirrored image of systemic bias instead of intrinsic benefit.

This phenomenon, known as historical bias, is compounded through representational bias, which takes place whilst sure populations are underrepresented or misrepresented in education information. Facial popularity systems, as an example, were shown to perform appreciably worse on people with darker pores and skin tones, in large part due to the fact the datasets used to train them comprise a disproportionate number of light-skinned faces. The outcomes of such bias aren't trivial. In law enforcement, a misidentification by using facial recognition can lead to wrongful arrests, detentions, and criminal entanglements that disproportionately affect marginalized groups. In healthcare, algorithms trained primarily on facts from prosperous, white populations might also fail to appropriately diagnose or prioritize sufferers from one-of-a-kind demographic backgrounds, main to disparities in care and results.

Bias in AI additionally arises from the methods in which issues are framed and translated into computational phrases. Every set of rules displays a set of priorities—what to optimize, what to ignore, what to take into account a success. These selections are hardly ever cost-impartial. For example, against the law prediction algorithm might be designed to decrease false negatives (failing to are expecting a crime that occurs) at the rate of fake positives (predicting a criminal offense that does not arise). Such a trade-off may seem justifiable from a statistical perspective however has severe moral implications if it outcomes inside the over-policing of positive neighborhoods or the stigmatization of unique organizations. Moreover, the very act of quantifying complex social phenomena—including chance, protection, or worthiness—invites distortion. Human lives do no longer without problems reduce to information factors or opportunity ratings, and efforts to accomplish that regularly mirror and enhance dominant cultural assumptions.

The design of AI systems is deeply formed with the aid of the folks who build them. Developers convey their own views, studies, and blind spots to the introduction of algorithms. In a tech enterprise that remains predominantly male, white, and prosperous, this homogeneity can translate into systems that serve the pastimes and norms of a narrow demographic. This developer bias isn't constantly overt, but it is despite the fact that influential. It affects the whole thing from the selection of research inquiries to the interpretation of outcomes, the definition of fulfillment metrics, and the prioritization of functions. Efforts to diversify the AI workforce are therefore now not absolutely matters of inclusion or illustration; they're important for making sure that the systems being built mirror a broader variety of human stories and values.

Another critical source of bias in AI is institutional and systemic. Organizations regularly adopt AI tools to streamline selection-making in contexts inclusive of hiring, lending, insurance, and crook justice. Yet these establishments themselves may harbor structural inequalities. When AI structures are deployed in such environments, they hazard entrenching and legitimizing these inequalities beneath the guise of objectivity. For instance, if a financial institution has traditionally denied loans to candidates from sure neighborhoods, a loan approval set of rules trained on beyond records may also finish that applicants from those areas are inherently excessive-hazard. The system, far from being unbiased, will become a mechanism for perpetuating redlining—a practice once explicitly racist, now reborn in the language of statistical inference. These dynamics illustrate how bias in AI is often less about rogue algorithms and extra about the institutional contexts in which they perform.

Recognizing bias is a essential first step, but mitigating it calls for concrete interventions at a couple of degrees. One technique is through cautious dataset creation and curation. This consists of efforts to ensure demographic stability, correct for historical imbalances, and audit datasets for anomalies or gaps. Yet this is a frightening project. Real-international records is messy, complicated, and regularly proprietary. Moreover, the choice for inclusivity can conflict with issues approximately privateness, consent, and records minimization. Synthetic records technology, wherein synthetic datasets are created to augment underrepresented groups, gives a capacity solution however increases questions on authenticity and realism.

Another street involves algorithmic strategies designed to discover and decrease bias. These include techniques for pre-processing records, editing getting to know algorithms to be equity-aware, and put up-processing outputs to ensure fairness. While promising, such strategies regularly face alternate-offs among accuracy and equity, transparency and complexity. There is no time-honored definition of equity, and optimizing for one metric may also worsen any other. For example, equalizing false tremendous prices across organizations may also result in disparities in different performance metrics. Navigating these trade-offs requires not just technical talent but ethical judgment and stakeholder engagement.

The position of regulation and governance in addressing AI bias is turning into an increasing number of outstanding. Governments and regulatory bodies are beginning to develop frameworks for auditing and certifying AI systems, in particular in excessive-stakes domain names. The European Union's proposed AI Act, as an instance, classifies AI packages through risk stage and imposes strict requirements on those deemed excessive-danger, together with transparency, documentation, and human oversight. In the US, discussions around algorithmic duty are gaining traction at each nation and federal levels, with proposals for algorithmic impact tests, public disclosure mandates, and anti-discrimination safeguards. However, regulatory responses remain fragmented and uneven, and enforcement mechanisms are still evolving.

Public cognizance and advocacy have performed a essential role in bringing attention to the trouble of AI bias. Whistleblowers, journalists, and researchers have uncovered the flaws and harms of biased systems, regularly at amazing non-public and professional value. Figures like Joy Buolamwini, Timnit Gebru, and Cathy O'Neil have end up outstanding voices inside the fight towards algorithmic injustice, emphasizing the want for transparency, duty, and inclusive layout. Civil society corporations have advanced tools for network audits, impact assessments, and participatory design processes that center the voices of these maximum laid low with AI structures. These efforts underscore the importance of democratizing AI governance and empowering affected groups to form the technologies that have an effect on their lives.

Education and literacy are also key components of any lengthy-time period strategy to deal with bias. As AI will become more and more included into normal life, it's far essential that customers—whether or not people, institutions, or policymakers—recognize how those systems paintings, what their boundaries are, and how to query their outputs. This entails now not just technical knowledge however important questioning, moral reasoning, and ancient cognizance. Bias in AI isn't a worm in the machine; it's miles a replicate reflecting deeper social injustices. Addressing it calls for a dedication to fairness, a willingness to confront uncomfortable truths, and the courage to imagine opportunity futures.

Looking beforehand, the challenge of bias in AI will only develop more complicated. As systems grow to be extra self sustaining, multimodal, and integrated into decision-making infrastructures, the stakes of bias increase. Emerging technology like big language fashions, generative AI, and real-time surveillance gear present new vectors for bias, some of which can be tough to expect or control. Moreover, the globalization of AI development means that biases are not restrained to national obstacles; a biased device developed in a single context will have ripple effects across the world. International cooperation, pass-cultural speak, and shared moral commitments might be crucial to navigate this landscape.

The challenge of bias in AI isn't one that can be solved as soon as and for all. It is a continuous procedure of mirrored image, vigilance, and edition. It requires humility on the a part of developers, openness at the part of establishments, and empowerment on the part of groups. The aim isn't to build perfect structures—an impossible task—but to build systems which might be accountable, responsive, and aligned with our maximum ideals. In this attempt, bias isn't always simply a technical obstacle but a ethical test. It asks us who we are, who we value, and what sort of world we need to build. Artificial intelligence holds exquisite promise, but only if we confront its challenges with honesty, integrity, and a dedication to justice.

CHAPTER 2

Artificial Intelligence and Decision Making

2.1 AI's Decision-Making Processes

Artificial Intelligence (AI) has transcended conventional software program systems by using enhancing machines' capabilities to acquire facts, examine it, and make decisions primarily based on that statistics. The choice-making strategies in AI have evolved from merely following rules and algorithms to incorporating extra dynamic, studying-based totally, and custom designed approaches.

AI's selection-making strategies normally rely upon foremost components: data processing and modeling. This procedure may additionally contain each human-like studying techniques (consisting of deep mastering) and extra traditional rule-based totally strategies. AI interacts with its environment, processes information, and creates models from this facts to make decisions. The decision-making method in AI follows several key steps:

1. Data Collection: AI structures gather statistics from diverse assets, together with sensors, digital structures, consumer interactions, social media, and extra. This statistics is a fundamental useful resource for AI to understand its environment and perform actions.

2. Data Processing and Analysis: After information series, AI systems analyze the records the use of statistical methods, gadget gaining knowledge of algorithms, or deep gaining

knowledge of techniques. AI extracts meaningful insights from the statistics, predicts possible outcomes, or builds models vital for choice-making.

3. Model Development: Based at the processed statistics, AI creates a mathematical or statistical model. This model is skilled to expect future states or make selections that gain particular objectives. The version can be constructed the usage of strategies like linear regression, choice bushes, or neural networks.

4. Decision-Making and Application: Once the version is developed, AI makes decisions based on the predictions made by means of the version. These choices are commonly optimized thru a process, wherein AI selects the excellent direction of movement to gain a goal. AI then applies those selections to influence its environment.

Several key strategies are generally employed in AI's decision-making strategies:

1. Machine Learning (ML): Machine studying is a method that allows AI to study from statistics. In this method, a model is skilled with a dataset, and then examined on new, unseen data. Machine learning has subcategories like supervised getting to know, unsupervised gaining knowledge of, and reinforcement gaining knowledge of.

Supervised Learning: AI is skilled on categorized records and learns to predict an appropriate output for brand new information.

Unsupervised Learning: AI is given unlabeled data and reveals styles or systems inside the records, together with clustering.

Reinforcement Learning: AI learns through interacting with its environment, receiving remarks within the form of rewards and penalties, to optimize its selection-making.

2. Deep Learning: Deep getting to know, a subset of gadget learning, is especially powerful for dealing with massive datasets. Using artificial neural networks, deep gaining knowledge of permits AI to system complex records and make choices based totally on nuanced patterns. This technique is extensively used in packages like photo recognition and natural language processing.

3. Decision Trees and Random Forests: Decision trees are structures where each branch represents a circumstance, and the leaves constitute consequences or decisions. Random forests combine a couple of choice trees to improve prediction accuracy, ensuing in a greater reliable selection-making technique.

4. Genetic Algorithms: Inspired by natural selection, genetic algorithms look for foremost answers through evolving answers thru tactics inclusive of reproduction, mutation, and choice. AI uses these algorithms to discover various choices and enhance its selection-making through the years.

The effectiveness of AI's choice-making approaches is heavily influenced with the aid of the human aspect. Humans play a essential role in designing AI systems, guiding the selection-making strategies via considering moral, social, and cultural elements. The selections made by way of AI are formed via the input and oversight furnished through humans.

1. Data Labeling and Selection: Humans label and select the information used to educate gadget getting to know fashions. This procedure is important in making sure that the version learns to make correct decisions. Errors in records labeling or biased facts choice can cause fallacious outcomes from AI structures.

2. Algorithmic Bias: Humans have an impact on AI's choice-making via the biases inherent inside the facts they provide. If AI is educated on biased statistics, its choices can be skewed in want of certain agencies or views, resulting in unfair outcomes.

3. Ethical Decisions and Responsibility: Humans should also take into account moral responsibility while designing AI decision-making methods. AI may make selections that could be dangerous or risky to people, so it's far critical that choice-making is monitored and aligned with ethical standards.

The societal results of AI's decision-making procedures are growing more great. AI's have an effect on spans across numerous fields, including healthcare, finance, justice systems, and schooling. The choices made through AI may have profound affects on people, corporations, and groups. For example, in healthcare, AI's choice-making can at once affect affected person treatment plans. The following elements highlight a number of the important thing societal implications:

1. Social Inequality and Discrimination: AI decision-making strategies have the potential to exacerbate social inequalities. For example, AI-powered credit scoring structures might drawback people based on their financial records, perpetuating social and financial divides. Thus, it's miles critical for AI structures to be designed with fairness in thoughts, ensuring that they do not strengthen existing biases or inequalities.

2. Transparency and Accountability: AI's selection-making techniques can be complicated and hard to understand. This highlights the need for transparency and duty in how selections are made. Stakeholders, such as users and regulators, need to be capable of understand how AI reaches its conclusions and maintain it accountable for its moves.

AI's choice-making strategies are built upon advanced records evaluation and modeling strategies, growing dynamic and custom designed choice-making structures. The position of human involvement is important to make sure those systems function ethically and efficaciously, with duty and fairness. As AI continues to play an increasingly full-size role in numerous sectors, it's far critical to continuously refine and monitor those selection-making techniques to address societal worries and make sure fine outcomes for all.

2.2. AI and Its Impact on Humanity

Artificial Intelligence (AI) has emerged as one of the most transformative forces in human records. Its impact is felt across every zone, from healthcare and schooling to enterprise and enjoyment. As AI maintains to evolve, it is reshaping the manner people live, work, and interact with generation.

One of the most profound affects of AI on humanity is its capacity to reshape economies. As AI structures end up extra sophisticated, they're automating responsibilities traditionally achieved by way of people. In industries which includes production, transportation, and logistics, AI-powered machines can now whole repetitive, hard work-intensive obligations with pace and accuracy, lowering the need for human people. This has caused huge shifts in exertions markets, as ordinary jobs are replaced through automation.

While automation has the capacity to growth efficiency and productivity, it also increases worries approximately task displacement. Many people in low-skilled or routine jobs face the chance of losing their livelihoods as AI takes over their roles. For instance, independent motors may want to eliminate jobs for truck drivers, at the same time as AI structures in customer service may want to replace name middle personnel. The mission for society will be to control this transition, retraining people and making sure that the advantages of AI-driven productivity profits are dispensed equitably.

On the other hand, AI is also creating new possibilities for innovation and entrepreneurship. By enabling more customized offerings and automating complicated approaches, AI is opening up new enterprise avenues. Companies are leveraging AI to enhance decision-making, optimize supply chains, and beautify consumer experiences. In fields consisting of healthcare, AI is assisting inside the development of precision remedy, while in finance, it is assisting with chance assessment and fraud detection.

AI's affect extends beyond the economic sphere, impacting the social material of society. As AI structures grow to be greater included into daily existence, they may be reshaping how humans engage with one another and with era. Social media structures, for example, use AI algorithms to curate content material, influencing what users see and how they engage with records. These algorithms can create echo chambers, wherein users are exposed simplest to viewpoints that align with their present ideals, potentially deepening societal divisions.

AI is likewise affecting human relationships. With the rise of virtual assistants, chatbots, and AI-pushed conversation tools, human beings are increasingly more interacting with machines in preference to with different human beings. While

AI can offer comfort and performance, it additionally raises questions about the first-rate of human interplay and the capability for social isolation. In some instances, AI-powered companionship equipment, which includes social robots, are being advanced to address loneliness, however the ethical implications of replacing human relationships with machines continue to be contentious.

Furthermore, AI's potential to tune and examine personal information has raised issues approximately privacy and surveillance. AI-powered structures can acquire massive quantities of facts approximately individuals, from surfing behavior to physical locations. Governments and agencies are increasingly more the use of AI to screen populations, raising questions on the stability between protection and character rights. In a few instances, AI-pushed surveillance can be used for social control, as seen in authoritarian regimes, wherein it's miles used to suppress dissent and display citizens' activities.

AI is revolutionizing healthcare by enhancing diagnostics, personalizing treatment, and improving drug development. AI-powered algorithms can analyze medical facts which include photos, genetic facts, and affected person histories to identify patterns that may work neglected via human docs. This has the capability to noticeably improve diagnostic accuracy, especially in fields together with radiology, pathology, and oncology.

For instance, AI systems have validated the ability to hit upon positive sorts of cancer at an earlier degree than human docs, leading to higher outcomes for sufferers. In customized medicinal drug, AI is getting used to layout customized remedy plans primarily based on an character's genetic makeup, enhancing the effectiveness of remedies. Additionally, AI is assisting in drug discovery by way of predicting the efficacy of recent compounds and identifying ability facet effects before clinical trials start, decreasing the time and cost involved in bringing new drugs to marketplace.

Despite those advancements, the combination of AI into healthcare additionally increases concerns approximately the position of human clinicians. While AI can help medical doctors in making choices, it can not replace the human touch in affected person care. Trust among patients and medical doctors is important, and sufferers may sense uncomfortable with AI making life-altering selections without human oversight. Moreover, the use of AI in healthcare poses moral dilemmas regarding information privateness, consent, and the capability for algorithmic bias in scientific selection-making.

AI affords a number of moral and philosophical questions that humanity ought to grapple with because it maintains to adapt. One of the most pressing worries is the query of duty. When AI systems make choices that have extensive effects, inclusive of in self-using motors or crook justice algorithms, who is chargeable for the effects? Should the builders who created the AI be held accountable, or ought to the machines themselves undergo responsibility for their movements? The loss of clear criminal frameworks for AI selection-making complicates this issue and poses challenges for regulators.

Another moral problem is the capability for AI to reinforce or exacerbate current biases. AI structures are often educated on facts that displays historic inequalities, which include biased hiring practices or discriminatory policing. As a end result, AI can perpetuate these biases, main to unfair results for sure agencies of people. This difficulty has raised calls for expanded transparency and fairness in AI development, with the purpose of making structures which can be extra equitable and inclusive.

Furthermore, the speedy advancement of AI has sparked debates approximately the nature of intelligence and awareness. If machines can mimic human choice-making and research from enjoy, at what point do they emerge as more than simply equipment? Will AI ever gain a stage of awareness that makes it morally relevant, or will it continue to be a sophisticated shape of computation? These questions assignment our information of what it means to be human and our dating with the machines we create.

As AI keeps to enhance, its impact on humanity will most effective emerge as extra profound. On a worldwide scale, AI is predicted to play a primary role in fixing a number of the sector's maximum urgent challenges, consisting of climate trade, poverty, and ailment. AI systems can analyze big quantities of environmental statistics to model climate trade scenarios, optimize useful resource use, and expand answers for renewable power production. In global fitness, AI can assist music and are expecting sickness outbreaks, imparting well timed responses to public fitness crises.

However, AI also has the ability to exacerbate international inequalities. The international locations and organizations that increase and manage AI technology might also have disproportionate strength, doubtlessly leading to economic and political dominance. There are concerns that the blessings of AI will be concentrated inside the fingers of some, leaving developing nations and deprived populations in the back of. To ensure a more equitable destiny, global cooperation and law might be important in dealing with the global distribution of AI advantages.

The effect of AI on humanity is multifaceted, with both fine and bad consequences. While AI has the potential to revolutionize industries, improve healthcare, and address global challenges, it also increases large ethical, social, and economic concerns. The key to making sure that AI advantages humanity lies in how it is developed, regulated, and included into society. As AI continues to adapt, it is vital that we continue to be vigilant in addressing these challenges, ensuring that the technology serves the common true and enhances the first-rate of existence for all.

2.3. AI and Moral Issues

As Artificial Intelligence (AI) keeps to develop at an extraordinary charge, it raises a series of moral troubles that mission conventional standards of ethics, duty, and choice-making. The integration of AI into diverse sectors, from healthcare and crook justice to self sustaining cars and war, introduces questions about the moral duties of builders, customers, and society as a whole.

One of the maximum urgent ethical worries surrounding AI is the problem of responsibility. As AI systems become more self reliant and capable of making decisions without human intervention, it becomes increasingly difficult to decide who's answerable for the consequences of those decisions. For instance, if an self sustaining automobile reasons an coincidence, who need to be held in charge? The producer of the vehicle, the builders of the AI device, or the passengers who were operating the car? Similarly, within the case of AI-pushed algorithms used in crook justice structures that have an effect on sentencing or parole selections, who is accountable if the system's pointers cause unjust effects?

The undertaking of accountability is compounded by the opacity of many AI algorithms. Machine studying models, specifically deep gaining knowledge of systems, are often "black boxes," that means that even the developers may not fully apprehend how the machine arrives at its choices. This loss of transparency makes it difficult to assess the fairness and accuracy of AI structures, and it raises worries about the potential to keep entities chargeable for harmful actions. This trouble of responsibility is not handiest a prison task but additionally a ethical one, as it touches on questions of justice and fairness in society.

Another sizeable ethical difficulty with AI is the capability for bias and discrimination. AI systems are trained on massive datasets that mirror historic and societal styles. If those datasets include biases—whether or not in hiring practices, regulation enforcement, or lending—AI systems can perpetuate and even exacerbate those biases. For instance, predictive policing algorithms that use historical crime statistics may disproportionately goal marginalized groups, reinforcing systemic inequalities in the crook justice gadget. Similarly, AI-based hiring tools may also favor male applicants over female candidates if the schooling information is skewed toward male-dominated industries or process positions.

The ethical implications of AI bias are profound, as they can result in unfair and discriminatory consequences that negatively affect vulnerable populations. This raises questions about the moral duty of AI developers to make sure that their systems are truthful, obvious, and inclusive. It also highlights the significance of addressing the broader societal biases that are contemplated in AI records, as those biases aren't just technical problems however ethical ones that affect human beings's lives in widespread ways.

AI's ability to make decisions on behalf of human beings increases concerns about autonomy and human enterprise. As AI systems emerge as extra included into choice-making approaches, there may be a threat that individuals may lose manage over their personal lives and choices. For example, in healthcare, AI-pushed diagnostic gear might also make clinical decisions with out consulting patients, potentially undermining patients' autonomy in making informed selections approximately their own remedy. Similarly, in areas which includes finance, AI algorithms that routinely make funding choices ought to lessen individuals' capacity to control their financial futures.

The moral concern here is that, as AI will become greater succesful, it is able to erode human organisation through taking over decisions that had been formerly made by means of people. This increases essential ethical questions on the boundaries of AI intervention and the want to hold human autonomy. While AI can help in selection-making, it is important that it does no longer replace human judgment or undermine man or woman rights to make personal choices.

The deployment of AI in military applications introduces a in particular troubling set of moral issues. Autonomous guns structures, inclusive of drones and robots, are being developed with the capability to perceive and engage goals with out human intervention. While these systems can be visible as greater green or specific, additionally they enhance profound ethical issues approximately the position of AI in lifestyles-and-demise selections.

One of the principal ethical dilemmas is the capability for AI to make decisions about the use of pressure with out human oversight. In situations where AI systems are tasked with focused on and putting off perceived threats, there is the risk that they could make errors, main to unintended harm or civilian casualties. The loss of human empathy and judgment in these systems increases questions on the morality of allowing machines to decide who lives and who dies. Furthermore, autonomous weapons could be utilized in ways that violate worldwide humanitarian regulation, together with concentrated on non-combatants or accomplishing disproportionate force.

The use of AI in battle also affords challenges in phrases of responsibility. If an self sufficient weapon reasons damage or violates ethical ideas, it is unclear who have to be held responsible. The developer, the military, or the device itself? This ethical uncertainty underscores the want for clean policies and moral tips surrounding the usage of AI in military settings.

As AI keeps to strengthen, the question of gadget cognizance and rights becomes more relevant. While contemporary AI structures aren't aware and do no longer own feelings or self-recognition, the improvement of extra sophisticated AI may subsequently cause machines that show off behaviors such as focus. In such instances, ethical questions stand up approximately the rights of AI entities.

If an AI device were to end up aware, wouldn't it have ethical rights? Could it's taken into consideration a person in a felony feel, deserving of the same protections and privileges as humans? These are questions that philosophers and ethicists are grappling with as AI technology advances. While these concerns might also appear speculative at the moment, the rapid pace of AI improvement indicates that they will end up increasingly more pressing in the destiny.

The moral catch 22 situation right here isn't handiest about the rights of AI but additionally approximately our duties toward the machines we create. If AI structures can revel in struggling or have desires, we might also have an moral responsibility to deal with them with respect and care. This raises profound questions on the nature of focus, the ethical fame of machines, and the ability for a new shape of moral consideration inside the destiny.

Looking beforehand, the moral challenges posed by way of AI are probable to grow to be even more complicated. As AI systems grow to be more capable, self reliant, and included into society, they'll boost new moral dilemmas that have not begun to be absolutely imagined. The moral implications of AI will keep to evolve as generation progresses, and it is crucial that society engages with these troubles in a thoughtful and proactive manner.

The future of AI and morality will depend on how human beings pick to develop, regulate, and use AI. Ethical frameworks will want to be installed to make certain that AI systems are aligned with human values and that their deployment does not damage people or society. Moreover, AI developers, policymakers, and ethicists will need to collaborate to address the various ethical questions that AI increases, making sure that the technology is used responsibly and ethically.

The ethical troubles surrounding AI are tremendous and multifaceted, bearing on the whole thing from accountability and bias to autonomy, battle, and the capacity for machine consciousness. As AI maintains to shape the future, it's far critical that we approach these ethical questions with care and attention, making sure that AI serves humanity in a manner that upholds justice, fairness, and moral responsibility.

2.4. Explainable AI: Understanding Algorithmic Choices

As artificial intelligence becomes an an increasing number of embedded function of cutting-edge existence—informing economic choices, guiding clinical diagnoses, filtering facts on social media, and even influencing judicial effects—the opacity of its internal workings poses an pressing and far-reaching challenge. Among the critical standards emerging to confront this difficulty is explainable AI, often abbreviated as XAI, a area that seeks to render machine gaining knowledge of fashions extra transparent, interpretable, and in the end responsible. The middle question that motivates explainable AI is deceptively easy but philosophically and technically profound: how are we able to recognize and agree with selections made via structures whose common sense frequently escapes human comprehension?

Modern gadget mastering, particularly deep mastering, has made brilliant advances in duties including image reputation, language processing, and strategic game play. Yet these structures often operate as so-referred to as "black bins"— complex, multi-layered networks of computation in which inputs are transformed into outputs through non-linear interactions that defy intuitive knowledge. For instance, a deep neural community would possibly correctly classify a medical picture as cancerous, but be not able to articulate why it reached that conclusion in a manner that a radiologist—or a affected person—can hold close. This lack of interpretability turns into particularly troubling in excessive-stakes contexts in which selections bear tremendous consequences for human lives, livelihoods, or criminal status. In such instances, explainability is not a luxury; it's far a moral and frequently legal necessity.

The imperative for explainability stems from numerous overlapping worries. First is the want for accept as true with. Users are more likely to simply accept and undertake AI systems after they understand how and why selections are made. This is especially genuine in domain names like healthcare, where professionals are reluctant to depend upon opaque algorithms, and in finance, where regulators require that mortgage selections be traceable and justifiable. Second is the necessity of duty. When AI systems malfunction, make mistakes, or produce biased outcomes, identifying the source of the problem is essential for remediation and justice. Without explainability, responsibility becomes diffuse, making it hard to assign blame or accurate conduct. Third is the principle of autonomy. Democratic societies are founded at the perception that people have the proper to understand selections that have an effect on them and to venture the ones choices when necessary. Opaque AI structures can undermine this right by means of making it difficult or impossible to question, appeal, or even recognise the reason at the back of algorithmic judgments.

Yet in spite of its importance, explainability is a notoriously difficult intention to gain in practice. Part of the mission lies inside the inherent complexity of contemporary AI models. Deep studying structures, for example, can also include millions or maybe billions of parameters, organized in problematic layers that interact in distinctly non-linear methods. These architectures are optimized for accuracy, not interpretability, and their inner representations frequently lack clean semantic which means. Furthermore, the information used to teach these fashions may be high-dimensional, unstructured, or noisy, similarly complicating efforts to trace causal pathways or attribute selections to specific capabilities. The very techniques that make system learning effective— together with hierarchical characteristic gaining knowledge of and stochastic optimization—also make it opaque.

Another difficulty arises from the anomaly of what counts as an "clarification." Different stakeholders require one-of-a-kind types of understanding. A records scientist may need an in depth account of the internal mechanics of a version; a regulator may call for a justification that aligns with criminal norms; a patron might select a simple, intuitive rationale. These divergent desires create a anxiety among accuracy and comprehensibility. Simplifying a model to make it more interpretable may additionally sacrifice predictive power, even as maintaining complexity can also alienate or confuse users. There is no accepted definition of explainability, and efforts to offer motives frequently contain exchange-offs among constancy to the version's common sense and accessibility to human reasoning.

Despite these challenges, researchers have developed lots of strategies to improve the interpretability of AI systems.

Some strategies focus on building inherently interpretable fashions—such as choice bushes, linear regression, or rule-based systems—whose structure is transparent with the aid of design. These fashions are easier to explain, but can be much less able to capturing complex patterns in the data. Other processes intention to extract reasons from complex models put up hoc. These include methods like LIME (Local Interpretable Model-agnostic Explanations), which approximates a complicated version with a simpler one around a particular prediction, and SHAP (SHapley Additive exPlanations), which assigns significance rankings to every characteristic based on sport-theoretic principles. Visualizations, consisting of saliency maps in picture category or interest weights in herbal language processing, offer every other manner of insight with the aid of highlighting which elements of the input information maximum inspired the model's selection.

These strategies have proven promise, but additionally they include limitations. Post hoc explanations won't mirror the proper internal workings of the version, raising questions about their validity. Saliency maps can be noisy or deceptive, and attention weights do no longer usually correlate with causal affect. Moreover, causes that rely upon complicated statistical ideas may still be unintelligible to put users, defeating the purpose of creating AI greater handy. There is a developing reputation that explainability isn't always merely a technical assignment, however a socio-technical one. It includes not just algorithms, but human beings—what they want, what they apprehend, and what they agree with. This perception has caused a shift in the direction of human-centered explainability, which emphasizes the layout of explanations which can be tailor-made to the cognitive and contextual needs of users.

The importance of explainable AI becomes mainly acute in contexts where selections intersect with criminal or ethical norms. In the European Union, for example, the General Data Protection Regulation (GDPR) includes a provision that a few interpret as a "right to clarification"—the idea that individuals have a right to understand the common sense behind automated decisions that notably have an effect on them. While the appropriate scope of this right remains contested, it signals a broader felony and normative fashion towards stressful transparency from algorithmic structures. In the US, regulatory businesses including the Federal Trade Commission have began to explore policies that would require agencies to disclose how their algorithms paintings, specifically in regions like credit score scoring, hiring, and housing. These trends replicate a developing focus that explainability isn't always just a matter of first-rate practice but a requirement for compliance with democratic norms and human rights.

The demand for explainability also intersects with worries about fairness and bias. Without perception into how a version makes decisions, it becomes tough to detect or correct discriminatory consequences. A hiring set of rules, as an instance, might look like neutral, however in practice may be filtering out applicants from underrepresented backgrounds based totally on proxy variables which include zip code or faculty attended. Explainability can assist reveal those hidden correlations and provide a basis for auditing and remediation. However, the presence of an explanation does now not guarantee that the machine is honest or just. Explanations can be used to rationalize biased choices or difficult to understand structural inequalities. They can create a false feel of protection or legitimacy. Thus, explainability need to be coupled with critical scrutiny and moral mirrored image.

In the area of device gaining knowledge of studies, there is an ongoing debate approximately whether or not complete transparency is even possible or desirable. Some argue that complex fashions are inherently inscrutable and that efforts to pressure interpretability may additionally constrain innovation. Others contend that interpretability is a precondition for accountable deployment and that systems whose selections can not be understood should not be trusted. Still others suggest for a middle direction, emphasizing context-based explainability—where the extent and form of explanation are tailor-made to the specific application and audience. For instance, a physician the usage of an AI diagnostic tool can also need one of a kind factors than a software engineer debugging the model, or a affected person searching for reassurance approximately a medical recommendation.

These debates have additionally spurred hobby within the epistemological and philosophical foundations of explainability. What does it mean to "apprehend" a version? Is information a remember of being capable of simulate the model's conduct, to are expecting its outputs, to grasp its internal logic, or to situate it inside a broader causal narrative? How will we balance formal rigor with intuitive accessibility? And who gets to determine which explanations are desirable? These questions display that explainability isn't always simply a technical intention however a deeply human one. It touches on our conceptions of expertise, employer, and responsibility. It challenges us to reconsider the bounds between human and system reasoning.

Explainability is also a dynamic belongings. A model this is interpretable today can also grow to be opaque the next day as new data, contexts, or customers input the picture. Continuous tracking, updating, and user comments are vital to hold relevance and believe. Moreover, as AI structures evolve to comprise factors such as reinforcement getting to know, unsupervised learning, or multi-agent interplay, the task of explanation grows. How can we give an explanation for a machine that learns in real time, adapts to user conduct, or coordinates with other self reliant marketers? These aren't hypothetical issues; they may be increasingly salient in applications starting from personalized education to self sustaining motors and monetary trading.

In reaction to these demanding situations, interdisciplinary collaboration has grow to be essential. The subject of explainable AI now draws on insights from laptop technological know-how, cognitive psychology, philosophy, law, layout, and human-laptop interplay. This convergence displays the complexity of the challenge and the need for numerous views. Designing reasons that are accurate, meaningful, and ethically grounded calls for now not simplest technical talent however empathy, communique, and cultural cognizance. It requires engaging with cease-customers, information their desires and issues, and iteratively refining explanatory interfaces. It additionally calls for institutional assist, which includes resources for schooling, oversight, and public engagement.

The destiny of explainable AI will probable involve a shift from static motives to interactive, dialogic systems. Rather than supplying one-length-fits-all rationales, AI systems could interact customers in conversations, adapting motives to their questions, possibilities, and degree of information. Such systems might function extra like instructors or collaborators than static equipment. They could foster know-how thru dialogue, not monologue. They might empower users to invite "what if" questions, discover alternative scenarios, and increase mental models of ways the gadget works. Achieving this imaginative and prescient will require advances in herbal language generation, consumer modeling, and cognitive technology. But it also calls for a dedication to transparency as a essential layout aim.

Explainable AI is a critical and multifaceted area at the intersection of technology, ethics, and society. It addresses the essential need to recognize how selections are made, to consider the structures that affect our lives, and to hold those structures responsible. It demanding situations us to transport beyond narrow definitions of performance and to remember the wider human context in which AI operates. As algorithms retain to form our global, the query of explainability will most effective come to be greater urgent. Whether in the court docket, the lecture room, the health center, or the public rectangular, the ability to apprehend and interrogate algorithmic selections is essential to retaining the values of equity, autonomy, and democracy. In a international an increasing number of governed by code, the demand for factors is a demand for dignity.

2.5. Human-in-the-Loop AI: Ensuring Oversight

The integration of artificial intelligence (AI) into choice-making strategies that have an effect on individuals, societies, and worldwide systems necessitates a careful stability among automation and human judgment. This balance is encapsulated inside the idea of "Human-in-the-Loop" (HITL) AI — a model in which people remain relevant to the functioning and control of clever structures. While completely independent AI structures are attractive because of their performance and scalability, their opacity, ability for blunders, and ethical implications highlight the want for human oversight. Human-in-the-loop AI serves as a guard in opposition to unchecked algorithmic conduct, allowing the incorporation of context, empathy, and ethical judgment in complicated decisions.

At its center, HITL refers to a gadget design wherein human beings are actively involved in the choice-making technique of AI. This involvement can range from preliminary training data labeling, actual-time oversight throughout operation, to put up-decision assessment. The presence of a human permits responsibility, provides nuanced know-how that may elude machine studying models, and guarantees that results align with societal values. It bridges the gap among black-container algorithmic choice-making and human ethical and contextual reasoning, mainly in high-stakes applications which include healthcare, crook justice, navy operations, economic systems, and self reliant cars.

In supervised device mastering, people are historically involved in labeling education data, a foundational segment in version development. However, as systems develop more sophisticated, HITL has accelerated past schooling into the deployment stage. One of the most widely followed models of HITL includes actual-time human oversight — for example, in scientific diagnosis systems, where AI suggests potential outcomes however a physician makes the final choice. In navy drone operations, no matter semi-self sufficient focused on talents, human operators usually authorize moves which include missile launches. This version maintains human ethical business enterprise, serving as a bulwark towards delegating lifestyles-and-demise decisions to machines.

Yet the implementation of HITL is not with out demanding situations. One main issue is the "automation bias," in which people overly rely upon AI outputs, diminishing their important oversight. Studies in aviation, medication, and regulation enforcement have shown that operators can also defer to algorithmic hints even if they contradict instinct or schooling. This undermines the motive of HITL, doubtlessly exacerbating dangers as opposed to mitigating them. To deal with this, HITL systems need to be designed to foster healthy skepticism, transparency, and energetic engagement rather than passive monitoring.

Another key situation lies in scalability and velocity. AI structures often characteristic in actual-time environments requiring split-second choices. In such contexts, the mixing of human oversight may also introduce latency. Autonomous motors navigating busy intersections, for instance, won't have enough money the luxury of human deliberation at some stage in every choice. Here, a tiered oversight version may be used: the AI handles habitual or time-important obligations autonomously, while people supervise exceptions, side instances, or submit-movement evaluate. This dynamic version of HITL recognizes the constraints of each human and gadget, combining their strengths for ideal performance.

HITL is particularly critical within the domain of algorithmic equity. Machine studying structures skilled on biased or unrepresentative statistics can perpetuate discrimination. Human oversight permits for vital inspection of effects, detection of bias, and recalibration of models. In credit scoring, as an example, algorithms might also inadvertently discriminate primarily based on zip codes or education stages, proxies for race or socioeconomic popularity. With a human inside the loop, such styles can be identified and corrected. Moreover, human reviewers can don't forget mitigating occasions that AI may not understand, which includes recent process loss or medical emergencies whilst evaluating mortgage packages.

In cybersecurity, HITL models are an increasing number of used in danger detection and incident response. AI can rapidly experiment community site visitors and discover anomalies, however interpreting those anomalies and figuring out whether or not they represent legitimate threats often requires human understanding. Human analysts examine the context, compare risk intelligence, and make informed selections approximately a way to reply. This partnership enhances each the accuracy of detection and the effectiveness of defense strategies, mainly towards novel or adaptive threats that may not be represented in historical datasets.

In the area of content material moderation, particularly on social media systems, HITL structures play a critical function. AI may additionally flag potentially dangerous or offensive content primarily based on sample reputation and keyword detection, however human reviewers examine the context to determine whether or not content truely violates platform recommendations. This is in particular essential in distinguishing satire from hate speech, or legitimate grievance from harassment. HITL hence helps a extra nuanced technique to moderation, protecting freedom of expression while maintaining safety and appreciate inside virtual spaces.

The clinical area offers one of the maximum effective examples of HITL in movement. AI-assisted radiology, as an instance, uses pc imaginative and prescient to hit upon tumors or fractures in clinical imaging. However, the final diagnosis and remedy plan is determined by way of a human radiologist who combines AI findings with patient records, scientific expertise, and expert judgment. This synergistic relationship improves diagnostic accuracy, reduces workload, and accelerates service shipping whilst retaining affected person safety.

Human-in-the-loop AI also has prison and regulatory implications. Certain jurisdictions are developing frameworks that mandate human oversight for precise classes of algorithmic decision-making. The European Union's AI Act, as an example, proposes obligatory human oversight for high-threat AI packages, which include the ones utilized in hiring, law enforcement, or biometric identity. These rules purpose to preserve human dignity, accountability, and recourse mechanisms. They additionally spotlight the need for structures that permit human intervention, auditability, and comprehensibility — reinforcing the centrality of HITL in responsible AI development.

However, the practical deployment of HITL raises questions about obligation and liability. When a gadget fails, who is responsible — the human operator, the AI developer, or the employer deploying the system? If human beings are simply rubber-stamping algorithmic selections, the veneer of oversight may additionally emerge as meaningless. Thus, effective HITL requires clean definitions of roles, obligations, and choice authority. Training is likewise essential: operators need to recognize how AI capabilities, its barriers, and the way to correctly interfere.

Moreover, the cultural size of HITL ought to no longer be not noted. Different societies may have varying thresholds for accept as true with in automation and different expectations of human organisation. For instance, in excessive-context cultures where choice-making is relational and context-touchy, there may be a extra emphasis on human judgment than in cultures that prioritize efficiency and standardization. This affects how HITL systems are perceived, followed, and operationalized. Designers need to be culturally conscious and adapt structures to reflect local norms, expectancies, and values.

A promising frontier in HITL is the concept of "meaningful human manipulate" — an evolution of oversight that emphasizes not simply presence, but empowerment. Meaningful human manage includes that human beings understand the AI machine, have the capability to override or accurate it, and are engaged in a context where their intervention has real consequences. This requires explainable AI, consumer-pleasant interfaces, robust remarks loops, and chronic education. It transforms human oversight from a procedural requirement into a significant guard.

The future of HITL may also involve even more sophisticated interplay models, which includes adaptive human-AI teaming. In this model, AI structures research from human comments and evolve in partnership with customers, even as people modify their workflows and mental models based on AI insights. Such systems require mutual transparency, accept as true with calibration, and shared intellectual fashions — a level of collaboration comparable to a co-pilot in place of a manager. This paradigm guarantees greater resilience, creativity, and performance in dynamic environments.

Human-in-the-Loop AI is not merely a technical architecture however a philosophical and ethical commitment. It reflects a notion inside the irreplaceable value of human judgment, obligation, and empathy. By embedding people inside the layout, deployment, and oversight of AI systems, HITL guarantees that automation serves humanity in preference to overrides it. As AI keeps to increase into every facet of existence, preserving human agency via thoughtful, accountable oversight will become now not only a fine practice, but a moral vital.

2.6. AI in Autonomous Systems: Ethical Dilemmas

Autonomous systems powered by artificial intelligence have converted industries and redefined human-machine interaction. From self-driving motors to automated drones, self reliant weapon structures, robot surgeons, and intelligent deliver chain managers, those structures promise unparalleled efficiency, responsiveness, and independence from direct human intervention. However, autonomy introduces new layers of ethical complexity. When machines are entrusted with making consequential decisions—every now and then with life-or-demise implications—the ethical panorama shifts dramatically. This bankruptcy delves into the intricate moral dilemmas posed by way of AI in autonomous structures, exploring responsibility, responsibility, transparency, safety, and the tension among technological development and human values.

At the middle of these moral challenges is the delegation of choice-making. When a self-using automobile have to pick out between shielding its passengers or pedestrians, whilst a army drone determines a goal with out human confirmation, or whilst an self reliant trading machine crashes a market—who is accountable? Is it the programmer, the facts teacher, the organisation, or the machine itself? Unlike conventional tools, autonomous systems do not simply execute pre-described instructions; they perceive, reason, and act, often in unpredictable methods. This capability for organisation, but restrained or probabilistic, forces a rethinking of our moral frameworks and criminal doctrines.

One of the maximum outstanding moral dilemmas lies in the vicinity of independent cars. The so-called "trolley trouble" has grow to be emblematic: need to an self sufficient vehicle swerve to keep away from hitting five pedestrians on the price of crashing and killing its passenger, or stay the direction and kill the 5? Although this scenario may additionally appear contrived, actual-life equivalents are inevitable. Engineers and ethicists ought to grapple with the way to encode moral choice-making into software. Moreover, those choices are further complex via the legal and cultural contexts wherein the systems function. What may be considered an acceptable trade-off in one country might be ethically impermissible in another.

The opaque nature of deep getting to know algorithms provides every other layer of moral difficulty. Many self sufficient structures perform as "black bins," making it tough to interpret how or why a particular choice became made. In high-stakes domain names consisting of healthcare or aviation, this lack of explainability undermines believe and accountability. For example, if an independent surgical robotic makes an error for the duration of a process, how can we trace the cause? Was it a defective sensor, an ambiguous dataset, or an unforeseen situation outdoor its schooling distribution? The incapacity to reconstruct a clean causal chain of reasoning hinders legal responsibility attribution and demanding situations regulatory oversight.

In military contexts, the usage of independent guns—frequently called Lethal Autonomous Weapons Systems (LAWS)—increases profound ethical and geopolitical questions. Can a device reliably distinguish among opponents and civilians in a dynamic battlefield? Can it interpret human intentions, give up signals, or contextual cues? Critics argue that the delegation of lethal force to machines undermines the concepts of worldwide humanitarian regulation and human dignity. The risk of unintentional escalation, algorithmic bias, and dehumanization of battle amplifies the stakes. Many professionals and advocacy businesses, along with the Campaign to Stop Killer Robots, have called for preemptive bans on LAWS, even as others propose for strict human oversight mechanisms. Yet, the attraction of pace, performance, and tactical benefit maintains to drive army investment in these structures.

Ethical dilemmas are also present in non-deadly domains. Consider self sufficient drones utilized in catastrophe alleviation or environmental tracking. While they could reach regions inaccessible to human beings, their information-accumulating abilities can also infringe upon privateness rights. Similarly, AI-pushed robot caregivers for the elderly or disabled can enhance pleasant of life but may foster emotional dependency, reduce human touch, or inadvertently overlook moral nuance in caregiving. In these kinds of cases, designers must count on now not most effective purposeful consequences however also the human values and social contexts stricken by their structures.

Accountability stays a primary challenge. Traditional criminal structures are predicated on the belief of organization and rationale—qualities that machines lack. When an self reliant machine malfunctions, determining liability turns into difficult. Should producers be held strictly answerable for all actions taken via their structures? Or ought to we recollect a dispensed model of duty, encompassing builders, facts curators, regulators, and customers? Legal scholars have proposed frameworks such as "algorithmic corporation," "vicarious legal responsibility," and "strict legal responsibility with insurance buffers," but consensus remains elusive. The hole among technological functionality and criminal infrastructure maintains to widen, stressful interdisciplinary cooperation.

Bias and discrimination are similarly complications. Autonomous structures skilled on historic information can mirror and make bigger social inequalities. For example, an autonomous hiring system would possibly discover ways to select male candidates primarily based on biased education statistics. An self reliant safety drone would possibly disproportionately goal humans of shade because of patterns in surveillance inputs. These moral disasters aren't simply technical errors—they mirror deeper societal problems encoded into algorithms. Transparency, equity, and auditability have to be built into the design of these structures from the outset. Furthermore, moral AI calls for numerous teams, inclusive datasets, and strong evaluation metrics that prioritize human well-being over performance on my own.

Another essential difficulty is cost alignment. Autonomous systems frequently optimize for precise objectives—fuel efficiency, target precision, transport pace—however may additionally overlook broader human values which include empathy, justice, or compassion. A transport drone can also prioritize the quickest route with out thinking about noise pollution in residential neighborhoods. A predictive policing algorithm may also maximize crime reduction on the rate of civil liberties. These change-offs aren't simply technical—they may be moral choices that require ethical foresight. Developers should interact stakeholders, ethicists, and communities to make certain that AI systems are aligned with the values of the societies they serve.

The deployment environment additionally plays a pivotal function in shaping moral results. A fully independent system working in a controlled factory ground presents fewer moral dangers than one navigating complex public areas. Context-attention, environmental sensing, and moral reasoning need to therefore be tailor-made to the particular domain. Adaptive systems that could amplify to human operators in ambiguous conditions—known as "human-on-the-loop" or "human-in-command" architectures—provide one pathway to mitigating moral dilemmas. However, those designs should also account for latency, operator overload, and the hazard of automation bias—wherein human beings defer to system judgments even when they're incorrect.

International cooperation and law are crucial. Autonomous systems, particularly in regions like aviation, transport, and our on-line world, frequently function across borders. Fragmented policies can create loopholes, inconsistencies, and enforcement challenges. Establishing global norms, safety requirements, and ethical benchmarks requires collaboration amongst governments, industries, academia, and civil society. Bodies which includes the IEEE, ISO, and UNIDIR have proposed ethical suggestions, however enforceable frameworks continue to be constrained. A coordinated method is necessary to make certain that independent AI structures do now not undermine fundamental human rights or democratic principles.

Education and public engagement are similarly crucial. Ethical dilemmas in AI are not solely the area of experts; they affect society at huge. Public attention, democratic deliberation, and participatory layout techniques can assist form the ethical trajectory of self sufficient technologies. Citizens have to have a voice in determining how those systems are utilized in public areas, healthcare, transportation, and justice. Transparency reviews, algorithmic audits, and civic technology initiatives can beautify duty and agree with.

The rise of self sustaining structures powered with the aid of artificial intelligence gives both huge promise and profound ethical dilemmas. As machines benefit the ability to perceive, determine, and act independently, humanity have to confront new questions about duty, equity, protection, and ethical corporation. These demanding situations can't be solved by engineers on my own; they require an interdisciplinary, inclusive, and globally coordinated reaction. Ethical frameworks have to evolve in tandem with technological progress to make sure that autonomy serves, in place of subverts, human values. Only then can we realize the full ability of self sufficient AI while safeguarding the standards that define our shared humanity.

CHAPTER 3

Artificial Intelligence and Responsibility

3.1. The Legal Status of AI

Artificial intelligence (AI) has rapidly emerged as a transformative technology, substantially changing the methods in which people and societies operate. However, the potential of AI is going past simply technological innovation; it also brings forth critical criminal, moral, and societal questions. The felony repute of AI is one of the key issues that arises with the development of this era, and how criminal frameworks evolve to address it's going to shape future traits.

To address the felony popularity of AI, it is essential to outline what is considered "felony" with regard to AI. Until now, AI has usually been dealt with as an "item" or "tool," that means that AI itself has no longer been held legally accountable. This places the duty on the designers and users of AI systems. As AI systems turn out to be more self reliant and complex, this traditional approach is proving to be inadequate.

The criminal repute of AI has emerge as a complex issue that calls for the integration of AI into existing legal systems. The law, at a sure point, might also battle to assign responsibility because AI could make choices and carry out responsibilities autonomously. This increases crucial questions about how the criminal consequences of AI's moves have to be assessed.

The prison identification of AI has evolved from being simply a set of software and algorithms to something a ways greater sophisticated. Today, a few AI structures are so advanced that they could perform independently and make choices primarily based on their personal getting to know approaches. This characteristic makes it an increasing number of difficult to deal with AI simply as a "device," and in some cases, the query arises as to whether AI itself must have a felony identity. For instance, if an AI system causes damage because of malfunction or makes an wrong selection, who have to be held accountable—its creators, its customers, or the AI itself?

In many nations, to deal with those criminal ambiguities, duty is often attributed to the designers and users of AI systems. However, these duties can be difficult to outline, especially on account that AI continues to adapt in approaches that make it unpredictable. As AI structures learn and adapt, their conduct won't be totally foreseeable, complicating the allocation of responsibility for his or her actions.

Another vast area of AI's legal implications pertains to contracts. Today, AI software is increasingly more used to create and put in force diverse commercial agreements, financial transactions, and prison files. This increases the question of whether a settlement created via AI holds the same felony weight as one created through a human. In many jurisdictions, the validity of a agreement created by way of AI is still a rely of debate.

For example, if an AI system creates a settlement between a service issuer and a user, would that contract be considered legitimate inside the present felony frameworks, or would it not best be valid inside the eyes of the AI's creators? Furthermore, how should criminal frameworks be designed to display and regulate AI's role in agreement advent and enforcement to make sure that those techniques are fair and obvious?

While AI is widely used to decorate productivity and decrease human errors in many industries, it also introduces criminal liabilities. For instance, if an AI gadget malfunctions or makes an wrong decision that causes damage or damage, who have to endure the financial responsibility? AI's involvement in selection-making, especially when its moves cause damage, raises crucial prison questions.

Liability for AI-triggered harm is typically directed closer to the designers or users of the device. However, as AI will become greater self sufficient and impartial, determining legal responsibility will become more complex. The criminal framework should recall the possibility that AI structures could make decisions outdoor of human manipulate, which may additionally require a rethinking of ways liability is assigned.

Legal regulations surrounding AI are nonetheless of their infancy and vary extensively across countries. However, as AI continues to increase, many nations are beginning to introduce legal guidelines that govern the use of AI. For instance, the European Union has taken steps to create law addressing the ethical use of AI and its compatibility with human rights and essential freedoms.

However, those rules regularly fail to embody all uses of AI. For instance, AI's utility in military settings, healthcare, or the monetary sector can also require particular, tailor-made regulations. The diverse programs of AI mean that felony frameworks have to be adaptable to cope with the nuances of each sector. For example, a prison framework governing AI in healthcare can also want to bear in mind privacy legal guidelines, clinical ethics, and the safety of sufferers, whilst in finance, worries over market manipulation and transparency are more generic.

The legal status of AI stays a growing area of debate worldwide. The steps taken on this area will not best impact generation businesses but also governments and lawmakers who must navigate the complexities of regulating this powerful device. As AI generation continues to evolve, there'll need to be a huge-based totally debate and coverage development to decide how AI can be incorporated into the criminal system.

Creating a criminal framework for AI that is able to addressing each the benefits and risks posed by using this technology might be important in ensuring that AI's ability is completely found out without undermining social and ethical standards. A multifaceted method to the prison fame of AI could be critical, as this era affects a huge variety of areas—from privacy and protection to economic markets and healthcare.

As AI structures keep to evolve, the obligation for their actions and decisions will need to be truely described. This duty will not only fall at the designers and customers of AI but additionally on society as an entire, which should make sure that legal structures evolve alongside these technologies to guard the commonplace desirable.

3.2. Responsibility: Machine or Human?

The question of duty in the context of artificial intelligence (AI) is a profound and complicated issue that has captivated criminal, moral, and philosophical debates in current years. As AI systems end up extra autonomous, their selections more and more effect human lives. However, as these structures perform without direct human manipulate, the quandary of assigning obligation turns into increasingly more challenging. Should the obligation for moves taken by way of an AI fall at the system itself, its creators, or the users of the gadget? This question touches upon fundamental problems in law, ethics, and generation, and requires careful exam of each human and machine organization.

Historically, obligation for actions has continually been positioned on humans—individuals or companies who are capable of making conscious decisions. In the case of AI, obligation traditionally rests with the human actors worried in the layout, improvement, deployment, and utilization of the generation. The creators of AI structures, for example, are predicted to take accountability for the design and function of the structures they increase, ensuring that their creations function within appropriate moral and felony boundaries. Additionally, individuals and corporations that use AI are chargeable for the choices made with the assistance of AI.

One of the principle motives human responsibility is often emphasized in these contexts is that, despite the fact that AI structures can be capable of performing tasks autonomously, they may be nonetheless designed, programmed, and maintained through human beings. Thus, the argument is going, humans are in the long run liable for the abilities and limitations of AI, as well as the outcomes of its actions. However, the complexity and autonomy of current AI challenge the adequacy of this framework.

The possibility of assigning responsibility at once to machines is a contentious problem. AI systems—specially those based totally on device getting to know—can evolve over time via publicity to facts and reviews, making selections that may not were foreseen through their creators. For instance, in self-driving automobiles, AI structures make split-2d decisions that would contain lifestyles-or-death situations. If an self sustaining automobile makes a selection that results in an twist of fate, have to the car or its manufacturer be held accountable? Or, ought to the liability fall at the human person who initiated the vehicle's operation?

Supporters of device obligation argue that AI structures, in certain cases, need to undergo some duty for their actions, especially while their autonomy reaches a stage where they make independent decisions that have an effect on human lives. For instance, within the case of absolutely independent robots or automobiles, if the AI machine is capable of making its very own choices based on enter records and plays actions without direct human oversight, it may be argued that it ought to be held accountable for its conduct.

However, this position raises full-size issues. Unlike humans, machines lack the capacity for ethical reasoning and the capacity to recognize the effects of their actions. Machines perform based on pre-programmed algorithms and found out styles, which means that at the same time as they will act independently, they do no longer have the ability to make moral decisions within the equal manner human beings do. This increases questions on the equity and practicality of conserving AI systems without delay responsible.

Given that machines themselves lack the ethical reasoning abilities vital for moral choice-making, responsibility tends to be assigned to people who layout and build AI systems. Developers, manufacturers, and companies that deploy AI are often considered legally and ethically chargeable for the actions of AI structures. The function of builders and manufacturers is critical in making sure that AI structures perform correctly, responsibly, and ethically.

For example, inside the context of self sufficient automobiles, manufacturers should ensure that the algorithms governing automobile conduct are designed to prioritize protection and adhere to criminal standards. Similarly, developers are answerable for testing AI systems to prevent unexpected or harmful consequences. If an AI gadget causes harm because of a design flaw or fallacious use of facts, the manufacturer or developer can be held responsible for the damage brought on. This concept of "designer responsibility" aligns with traditional legal frameworks, which area duty on human actors chargeable for products and services.

However, this view also faces demanding situations. As AI systems turn out to be an increasing number of complex, the builders and producers may not constantly completely understand the decisions made by means of the AI, mainly in machine gaining knowledge of systems wherein the AI "learns" from substantial amounts of data. In such cases, the line among human obligation and machine behavior will become blurry.

Another key element of responsibility lies with the customers of AI structures. In many cases, users engage with

AI systems, directing them to carry out precise tasks. For instance, an AI-powered advice system on an e-commerce platform may additionally suggest merchandise based on consumer alternatives, but it's miles the person who in the end makes the buying decision. In the case of self reliant automobiles, the consumer may offer a destination however does not directly manage the car's moves.

While customers might not layout or program AI structures, they are regularly chargeable for how the structures are deployed and used. In this context, users need to make certain that they're the usage of AI systems in a responsible and moral way. If customers act negligently or exploit AI structures in dangerous ways, they will be held chargeable for any poor outcomes. For example, if an autonomous drone is used recklessly and causes harm, the operator may also bear the criminal results, despite the fact that the AI system was the one appearing the movement.

The developing complexity of AI systems, however, makes it hard for users to completely apprehend the decisions being made by means of the AI, specifically within the case of "black-box" models wherein the reasoning in the back of choices is not obvious. This loss of transparency complicates the venture of obligation to users, particularly if they're blind to the capacity dangers or moral problems associated with AI systems.

Given the growing complexity of AI structures and their increasing autonomy, the present legal frameworks for assigning obligation are now not enough. As AI keeps to enhance, new models of responsibility have to be evolved to cope with the particular demanding situations posed via self sustaining structures. These frameworks might also need to recall shared responsibility among machines, human builders, manufacturers, and customers.

Some professionals suggest the concept of "co-obligation," wherein AI structures, builders, and users share responsibility for the actions taken by means of AI. Under this model, AI systems would be held answerable for sure selections, even as humans—whether builders or customers—would additionally bear duty for the context in which AI is used and for ensuring that systems are designed and deployed ethically.

Additionally, as AI structures emerge as more autonomous, it is able to be vital to set up prison ideas that govern the delegation of obligation to machines. These concepts ought to consist of ensuring that AI structures are designed to prioritize protection, ethics, and duty, in addition to developing mechanisms for human oversight in instances in which the AI's decisions have significant results.

The question of duty—whether or not it lies with machines, human beings, or both—raises complex and fundamental troubles that have to be addressed as AI turns into an integral a part of society. While human responsibility remains a important aspect of AI ethics and regulation, the growing autonomy of AI structures challenges conventional frameworks and necessitates the improvement of recent methods to accountability. As technology keeps to adapt, society should consider the way to stability the position of machines in decision-making with the moral and legal duty of human actors.

3.3. Decision-Making and Ethical Choices

The intersection of artificial intelligence (AI) and choice-making brings forth severa ethical dilemmas that venture the bounds of human organization and morality. AI's ability to make decisions, regularly independently, introduces new dimensions of obligation and ethical consideration, raising vital questions on the nature of choice, autonomy, and responsibility.

At the middle of AI's selection-making procedure lies algorithms—mathematical fashions designed to research information, understand styles, and make predictions or take movements. Traditional AI systems rely upon rule-based algorithms, in which a fixed of predefined instructions dictates how choices are made. However, contemporary AI, mainly system learning (ML) and deep learning (DL) fashions, operates in another way. These fashions can "learn" from big amounts of information, adapt to new conditions, and make decisions primarily based on past stories instead of specific programming.

In device getting to know, the selection-making technique is not static however evolves over time. AI structures are educated on statistics, which permits them to perceive relationships, correlations, and patterns in the facts set. This method that AI could make predictions, carry out classifications, and take moves that humans won't be capable of foresee. However, whilst those structures are pretty green and able to dealing with giant quantities of facts, they regularly lack transparency—leading to worries about responsibility whilst an AI system makes an sudden or dangerous decision. In the context of ethical selection-making, the dearth of transparency is a crucial trouble, as it makes it tough to apprehend how and why an AI gadget arrived at a particular end.

The utility of AI to decision-making processes increases vital moral questions. How need to AI systems be designed to make certain that the selections they make align with human values? What moral frameworks can manual the decisions of AI in conditions wherein the outcomes have vast implications for people and society?

There are several moral tactics that can be applied to AI choice-making. These frameworks aim to make certain that AI structures remember moral standards and human welfare of their choices:

1. Utilitarianism: This ethical principle indicates that the proper choice is the only that maximizes basic happiness or well-being. In AI decision-making, a utilitarian technique would contain making picks that benefit the finest wide variety of humans, despite the fact that it approach sacrificing the pastimes of a few. For example, an AI system in healthcare may prioritize remedies for sufferers with the best probabilities of survival, doubtlessly leaving out sufferers with decrease possibilities. However, applying utilitarianism in AI structures is controversial, because it raises worries about equity and the treatment of minority or vulnerable businesses.

2. Deontological Ethics: Deontology focuses on adherence to guidelines, obligations, and rights in place of the outcomes of moves. In AI selection-making, this can imply making sure that AI systems make selections that recognize human rights, uphold equity, and avoid causing harm, irrespective of the effects. For example, AI structures in criminal justice or law enforcement would need to adhere to moral recommendations that shield individuals' rights, ensuring that selections made by using the AI do no longer violate due manner or lead to unjust consequences.

3. Virtue Ethics: Virtue ethics emphasizes the significance of developing accurate man or woman developments or virtues, together with compassion, honesty, and equity. In AI, this approach could contain designing systems that replicate

virtuous behaviors of their decision-making processes. For instance, an AI utilized in social services might be programmed to show off empathy in its interactions with individuals in want. However, distinctive feature ethics in AI poses challenges, as virtues are subjective and culturally based, making it tough to outline universally generic standards for AI conduct.

4. Care Ethics: Care ethics emphasizes the significance of relationships, empathy, and the properly-being of people. In the context of AI, a care ethics method might prioritize decisions that keep or beautify human dignity and defend susceptible people. An AI in a caregiving putting, consisting of supporting elderly humans, could be designed to prioritize the nicely-being of individuals, ensuring that their emotional and physical wishes are met with compassion.

While those ethical frameworks provide a basis for moral choice-making in AI, they may be not at the same time exclusive. In exercise, AI structures may additionally integrate aspects of multiple ethical theories, and their decisions may additionally want to be flexible, adaptable to context, and attentive to evolving instances.

One of the main challenges of AI choice-making is its inherent loss of transparency. Many AI structures, especially the ones based totally on deep mastering, function as "black containers," where the decision-making system is not without problems understood by means of human beings. This opacity provides ethical issues, specifically in excessive-stakes domains which include healthcare, crook justice, and finance, where choices can notably effect people' lives.

To address this, the field of "explainable AI" (XAI) has emerged, specializing in growing AI systems that provide clear and understandable reasons for their selections. In order to make ethical alternatives, AI systems want to be explainable to both users and stakeholders, so that their selections can be scrutinized and held accountable. For instance, if an AI system is used in hiring, and it rejects a candidate, the candidate need to be able to understand why the decision became made— whether or not because of bias, loss of qualifications, or any other component. This transparency lets in individuals to task AI-driven decisions and ensures that the device operates pretty.

Explainability isn't always most effective important for accountability but also for accept as true with. Users are more likely to just accept AI decisions if they understand how those selections have been made, specifically whilst the ones selections affect their lives. Without transparency, AI structures can be perceived as arbitrary or unfair, leading to a lack of trust of their software and integrity.

As AI systems grow to be greater included into various components of existence, they unavoidably face conditions that gift ethical dilemmas. These dilemmas contain alternatives in which there may be no clean "right" solution, and the system must navigate competing values and interests. Some examples of moral dilemmas in AI selection-making include:

1. Autonomous Vehicles: When an self sufficient car encounters an unavoidable twist of fate situation, should the AI prioritize the safety of the passengers or the pedestrians? This traditional "trolley problem" increases hard questions on how AI have to make life-or-death selections, and what values must guide those selections.

2. Healthcare AI: In healthcare, AI systems may be tasked with making decisions approximately the allocation of confined assets, which includes ventilators or organ transplants. Should an AI system prioritize saving the lives of younger individuals with better survival costs, or ought to it don't forget other factors, along with the patients' high-quality of existence and contributions to society?

3. Criminal Justice: AI systems are increasingly more being utilized in predictive policing and sentencing. In those contexts, AI have to weigh the hazard of recidivism, the heritage of the offender, and societal pastimes. How can these structures keep away from perpetuating current biases and make certain fair consequences for all individuals worried?

4. Social Media Algorithms: AI-driven algorithms that endorse content material on social media structures face moral demanding situations in balancing freedom of expression with the prevention of dangerous content material, along with hate speech or misinformation. How ought to AI systems make

selections approximately what content ought to be promoted or suppressed, and to what extent need to user autonomy be respected?

These ethical dilemmas highlight the issue in programming AI structures to make morally sound selections, as well as the task of ensuring that AI choice-making aligns with societal values.

The intersection of decision-making and ethics in artificial intelligence represents one of the maximum considerable demanding situations inside the improvement and deployment of AI structures. As AI continues to strengthen, the choices made with the aid of those structures can have profound implications for individuals and society. It is crucial to create moral frameworks that guide AI choice-making, ensuring that the structures mirror human values, uphold equity, and shield human rights. Moreover, transparency and explainability ought to be prioritized to build agree with in AI systems and to ensure that their decisions can be understood, evaluated, and held responsible. As the sphere of AI continues to evolve, it's far important to have interaction in ongoing discussions approximately the moral implications of AI decision-making and to refine frameworks that balance the capabilities of AI with the ethical obligations that come with its use.

3.4. AI Accountability in Practice

Artificial Intelligence has transitioned from an experimental area into a pervasive pressure driving trade throughout sectors—from finance to healthcare, transportation to governance. With this change comes the growing recognition that AI systems, frequently making or influencing choices as soon as reserved for human beings, need to be held accountable. But accountability in AI is a complicated and multifaceted problem. It entails legal, technical, organizational, and moral considerations. Understanding how accountability operates in practice manner dissecting how duty is sent, how transparency is enforced, and the way redress mechanisms are carried out while AI systems reason harm. In this chapter, we explore what practical AI accountability seems like, the frameworks being developed to guide it, and the real-world challenges that preserve to complicate its application.

At its center, responsibility in AI refers back to the mechanisms and duties ensuring that builders, deployers, and users of AI systems are responsible for their actions and the effects of these structures. Unlike traditional technology, AI can show off self sustaining choice-making and opaque common sense, which makes tracing duty difficult. Nevertheless, in practical settings, accountability is about ensuring that systems perform in alignment with legal and ethical standards, and that there's recourse whilst those standards are breached.

One of the primary pillars of AI accountability is transparency. In realistic terms, transparency includes clean documentation of how an AI gadget changed into skilled, what statistics it used, what assumptions guided its design, and what risks have been taken into consideration. Organizations are an increasing number of required to create "model playing cards" and "records sheets" that accompany deployed structures. These artifacts function technical disclosures, detailing the AI machine's structure, schooling techniques, statistics sources, limitations, and anticipated conduct in extraordinary contexts. While such documentation doesn't resolve the opacity of deep studying fashions, it affords a foundation for assessing choices retrospectively and for auditing AI behavior.

Another practical layer of responsibility is auditing. Internal and external audits investigate whether or not AI structures observe regulatory and ethical requirements. Audits might also have a look at everything from bias and equity to performance degradation, interpretability, information privacy, and cybersecurity. Independent 1/3-birthday party auditors are regularly employed in high-danger domain names together with finance and healthcare. For example, banks using credit score scoring algorithms can face fines or reputational harm if their models reveal racial or gender bias. Auditors study historical decision logs, check facet cases, and examine statistical parity to become aware of intricate traits. Increasingly, regulators are pushing for obligatory effect tests and transparency reports—structured critiques of an AI gadget's societal implications, just like environmental effect reviews required for creation projects.

Accountability additionally demands a sequence of duty inside corporations. This involves absolutely defined roles for AI builders, product managers, prison advisors, and compliance officials. Just as in the case of data safety where the GDPR mandates the appointment of a Data Protection Officer (DPO), some regulatory frameworks are suggesting the appointment of AI Ethics Officers or Responsible AI Leads. These roles are designed to supervise the moral lifecycle of AI structures—from design and schooling to deployment and monitoring—and to behave as liaisons between technical groups and external stakeholders. When damage takes place or an AI system behaves all of sudden, it's far important to trace who was chargeable for every selection inside the development technique and what safeguards were in place.

Incorporating accountability into AI improvement pipelines is also approximately fostering a way of life of moral mirrored image and documentation. "AI Incident Reporting" is an emerging practice modeled after aviation and scientific fields, in which surprising results or near-misses are documented and shared anonymously to construct institutional information and save you recurrence. Initiatives together with the Partnership on AI's "AI Incident Database" encourage organizations to percentage information about screw ups or unintentional outcomes in AI structures. By gaining knowledge of from collective errors, the industry can build more strong systems and increase better requirements.

Legal liability is a key factor of responsibility in practice. When an AI system causes harm—which includes a self-riding car crashing right into a pedestrian—determining legal responsibility is a complicated assignment. Traditional prison systems are built around human actors and won't correctly seize distributed corporation. Jurisdictions are experimenting with prison units along with "strict liability" (preserving businesses liable irrespective of negligence) or "product legal responsibility" (treating AI as a faulty product). There is also dialogue round creating a separate criminal reputation for autonomous sellers, even though this stays controversial. The European Union's AI Act, for instance, introduces risk-primarily based law and places accountability squarely at the deployers of high-hazard AI systems, requiring documentation, hazard checks, and human oversight.

Practically speaking, corporations are responding to this moving legal panorama by building internal governance frameworks. These frequently consist of moral review boards, checklists for responsible AI, and education packages for builders. Companies like Google, Microsoft, and IBM have posted AI standards and created Responsible AI groups tasked with operationalizing them. However, critics argue that voluntary commitments are insufficient with out enforcement and outside scrutiny. Thus, multi-stakeholder tasks involving civil society, academia, and government are gaining momentum as collaborative governance fashions.

User-centric responsibility is every other vital practice. This approach making sure that quit-customers and affected people have clean approaches to contest AI choices and are trying to find redress. For example, within the realm of automatic hiring tools, candidates denied employment because of algorithmic choices must be informed approximately the logic in the back of the choice and be allowed to attraction or request human evaluate. In healthcare, sufferers subjected to diagnostic systems must be able to understand the prognosis intent and request second reviews. The concept of "meaningful human review" is now embedded in lots of regulations to save you full automation in excessive-stakes choices.

Monitoring and comments loops are critical for duty over time. AI systems aren't static—they research, update, and waft. Continuous monitoring guarantees that systems stay truthful, correct, and secure beneath converting situations. Model flow, antagonistic assaults, or accidental remarks loops can motive formerly trustworthy fashions to degrade. Organizations are imposing gear for overall performance logging, alert systems for anomalous behavior, and retraining protocols based on new data. However, this ongoing duty poses logistical and monetary challenges, in particular for smaller agencies.

Open-supply models and frameworks are contributing to practical duty through permitting peer overview and community scrutiny. When AI systems are proprietary and opaque, the general public has little way to assess them. But when models, datasets, and code are made public, they can be analyzed for fairness, protection, and integrity. Initiatives inclusive of OpenAI's documentation standards, Hugging Face's version cards, or Google's Responsible AI Toolkit provide sensible equipment for developers to make their systems more transparent and responsible from the outset.

Despite those improvements, real-world implementation of AI duty remains choppy. Many organizations lack the assets or incentives to absolutely engage in accountable AI practices. There is also a gap among coverage ambition and technical feasibility. For instance, implementing explainability in complicated neural networks remains an unsolved trouble, and differential privateness strategies—whilst promising—still include performance alternate-offs. Moreover, geopolitical fragmentation approach that duty standards vary throughout nations, creating loopholes and regulatory arbitrage possibilities for global agencies.

To support accountability in exercise, several steps are wished. First, harmonized global requirements could save you race-to-the-backside scenarios where companies perform inside the least regulated surroundings. Second, investment and support for smaller corporations to enforce responsible AI practices should be made available. Third, unbiased oversight bodies with enforcement powers—akin to financial regulators—must be installed to audit excessive-hazard AI structures. Finally, training and public literacy round AI ought to be advanced in order that customers, journalists, and civil society can seriously engage with AI choices.

AI accountability in exercise isn't merely a prison formality or a public members of the family tool. It is a foundational principle that guarantees technological development aligns with societal values and protects man or woman rights. From technical documentation and organizational roles to felony redress and user rights, accountability requires complete movement across the whole AI lifecycle. As AI systems emerge as extra succesful and embedded within the infrastructure of each day existence, the call for for obvious, enforceable, and significant responsibility mechanisms will best accentuate. Only by way of embedding these practices deeply into both technological and institutional layout are we able to ensure that AI serves the general public right in preference to undermines it.

CHAPTER 4

AI and Social Justice

4.1. AI and Social Inequality

As artificial intelligence (AI) keeps to evolve and combine into various facets of society, it is important to discover its implications on social justice, mainly in addressing issues of inequality. The ability of AI to transform economies, job markets, healthcare, and education brings with it an plain promise for development. However, with out careful consideration, the extensive implementation of AI may want to exacerbate present social disparities, amplifying social and economic divides. AI's role in perpetuating or mitigating social inequality increases several complex questions, ranging from algorithmic bias to the unequal distribution of technological assets.

AI has the electricity to either bridge or widen the distance among extraordinary socio-monetary organizations, relying on how it is designed and deployed. One of the core worries surrounding AI is its potential to perpetuate biases that exist within the facts it approaches. Since AI structures are regularly educated on massive datasets that replicate ancient patterns of human conduct, they are able to inadvertently adopt the biases present in these datasets. For example, if an AI system is used in hiring tactics and is trained on past hiring choices, it may replicate discriminatory patterns based totally on race, gender, or socioeconomic fame, leading to a loss of variety and perpetuation of systemic inequalities. This now not best affects the fairness of the system but also reinforces societal systems of privilege and drawback.

Moreover, the development and deployment of AI technologies are frequently concentrated in wealthier areas and international locations, this means that that get right of entry to to AI's advantages may be disproportionately available to prosperous populations. This disparity ought to lead to what some have referred to as a "virtual divide," where people from low-income or underrepresented groups are left at the back of, unable to get admission to the identical opportunities or sources as the ones in more privileged positions. The unequal get admission to to AI technology should bring about a in addition concentration of power and wealth inside the hands of a few, exacerbating international and neighborhood inequalities. For instance, in healthcare, AI structures that are expecting and diagnose medical situations may not be as effectively available in poorer regions, contributing to a disparity inside the nice of healthcare obtained by way of exceptional populations.

At the equal time, the utility of AI in social welfare structures, including predictive policing or welfare management, may be a double-edged sword. While these systems maintain the promise of enhancing efficiency and effectiveness in provider shipping, additionally they pose risks of reinforcing stereotypes and biases, particularly when they're now not carefully designed and monitored. AI in law enforcement, as an instance, has been criticized for disproportionately targeting marginalized groups, leading to racial profiling and unfair treatment. This no longer only affects the people directly concerned however also can result in broader societal implications, along with mistrust in public establishments and a loss of confidence in the equity of justice systems.

Addressing AI and social inequality calls for a multifaceted technique that prioritizes inclusivity, equity, and transparency inside the development and deployment of AI structures. Policymakers, technologists, and advocates for social justice should work collectively to ensure that AI does not emerge as a tool that entrenches existing inequities however as an alternative serves as a method to sell fairness and social progress. A key aspect of this attempt is ensuring that AI systems are designed with diverse datasets, loose from bias, and that they undergo normal audits to evaluate their impact on marginalized groups. Furthermore, equitable get entry to to AI technology have to be promoted to make certain that all people, irrespective of their social or monetary heritage, can enjoy the improvements AI has to offer.

The relationship between AI and social justice is complicated and requires ongoing exam. While AI holds the capability to address social inequalities, it also has the capability to deepen them if no longer carefully controlled. By prioritizing fairness, inclusivity, and transparency, society can paintings to make certain that AI technologies are a force for true in addressing social inequality, in place of a source of further department.

4.2. The Impact of AI on Humanity

Artificial intelligence (AI) has come to be a transformative force in cutting-edge society, influencing almost every element of human existence, from healthcare and education to enjoyment and communication. As AI technologies keep to improve, they may be reshaping the manner we work, interact, and understand the arena around us. While AI gives many possibilities for innovation and development, it additionally increases profound moral, social, and mental questions about its effect on humanity.

One of the maximum giant effects of AI on humanity is its impact on the job market and the destiny of work. AI technologies have already begun automating many tasks historically completed by way of human beings, particularly in industries inclusive of production, logistics, and customer service. While this automation can result in accelerated efficiency and reduced prices, it also raises issues approximately process displacement and the destiny of employment. Many people, in particular in decrease-skilled or repetitive roles, may additionally locate themselves liable to dropping their jobs as machines and algorithms take over their obligations. The shift towards automation ought to exacerbate profits inequality, with the ones in higher-skilled or generation-driven jobs profiting from AI advancements, at the same time as others face unemployment or underemployment.

In addition to the financial implications, AI is likewise changing the character of human interplay and social relationships. Social media systems, search engines like google, and advice structures powered via AI algorithms have emerge as deeply embedded in our each day lives. These systems form the records we consume, the humans we have interaction with, or even our political opinions. While AI can assist join people throughout the globe and offer customized hints, it is able to additionally make a contribution to the creation of clear out bubbles, wherein people are uncovered handiest to facts that aligns with their current beliefs. This can lead to increased polarization, the unfold of misinformation, and a decline inside the first-rate of public discourse.

Moreover, AI has the capability to affect human cognition and decision-making. With the upward thrust of AI-powered tools which includes virtual assistants, chatbots, and self reliant systems, human beings are an increasing number of relying on machines to carry out responsibilities that were as soon as within the realm of human intelligence. While this can boom convenience and efficiency, it additionally raises questions about how our dependence on AI might also alter our cognitive abilties. For instance, relying on AI for decision-making may want to reduce our capability for important thinking and hassle-solving, as individuals can also come to accept as true with AI's judgments over their personal. The growing reliance on AI to mediate our interactions and selections can also affect our potential to form meaningful connections with others, as we increasingly more interact with machines in place of with humans.

AI's effect on privateness and security is some other vital concern. As AI systems accumulate and analyze great amounts of personal records, inclusive of online conduct, clinical statistics, and social interactions, the capacity for misuse or abuse of this records will become a big chance. AI-powered surveillance structures, facial reputation technologies, and predictive analytics are being utilized in numerous sectors, from regulation enforcement to healthcare, raising issues approximately the erosion of privateness rights and the potential for surveillance-based social manipulate. The capacity of AI to tune people' moves, actions, and preferences should lead to a society in which private freedom is compromised, and individuals are constantly monitored and analyzed through machines.

Furthermore, the ethical implications of AI have become increasingly more complex as the generation advances. AI systems, particularly those utilized in high-stakes environments which includes healthcare and criminal justice, ought to make decisions that effect human lives. The capability for bias in AI algorithms—whether or not or not it's in medical diagnoses, sentencing in courts, or hiring practices—can perpetuate and exacerbate existing societal inequalities. AI has the capability to mirror and give a boost to the biases present inside the information it is trained on, leading to unjust consequences for marginalized communities. Ensuring fairness, duty, and transparency in AI structures is therefore crucial to save you discriminatory practices and shield the rights of people.

The relationship among AI and human identification is likewise a key vicinity of problem. As AI systems grow to be greater advanced, the line between human intelligence and gadget intelligence is turning into increasingly more blurred. The improvement of synthetic general intelligence (AGI)—machines that own the ability to recognize, study, and observe understanding in a way comparable to humans—raises questions about what it means to be human. If AI systems can mimic human notion approaches and behaviors, will they mission our information of focus, organisation, and personhood? This existential query opens up debates approximately the character of intelligence itself and the function that AI ought to play in human society.

Despite these concerns, AI additionally holds exquisite ability for improving human well-being. In healthcare, AI is already being used to assist in diagnostics, drug improvement, and personalized medicine, presenting the possibility of in advance disease detection and more effective treatments. In education, AI-powered tools can assist tailor mastering experiences to character students, enhancing consequences and addressing the various wishes of novices. AI also can beautify creativity via assisting artists, writers, and musicians of their creative strategies, presenting new possibilities for expression and innovation.

In order to ensure that AI blessings humanity in a truthful and equitable way, it is critical that we method its development and deployment with warning and foresight. Policymakers, ethicists, technologists, and the public ought to interact in ongoing discussions approximately the moral implications of AI and paintings together to create frameworks that sell transparency, responsibility, and fairness. By prioritizing human values and making sure that AI is utilized in ways that beautify, in place of lessen, our humanity, we are able to harness the electricity of AI to create a extra simply, equitable, and compassionate global.

As AI continues to evolve and combine deeper into our lives, its impact on humanity will surely hold to unfold. While AI presents both demanding situations and possibilities, it's far in the long run as much as us to decide how this effective technology will form the destiny of human civilization. With careful attention, ethical stewardship, and a commitment to social justice, we are able to make sure that AI serves as a tool for wonderful change, helping to create a extra inclusive, compassionate, and prosperous global for all.

4.3. The Future of Justice with AI

As synthetic intelligence (AI) maintains to adapt and its capabilities enlarge, it is increasingly more influencing sectors that historically depend upon human judgment, together with law, governance, and justice. The destiny of justice in an AI-pushed world holds terrific potential for reforming criminal structures, improving the equity of choice-making, and enhancing get right of entry to to justice. However, it also raises big moral, philosophical, and prison questions about the role AI have to play in ensuring justice and equity.

The incorporation of AI into the legal machine has already begun, with some countries experimenting with AI-pushed tools to help in felony studies, case evaluation, and even judicial selection-making. In the coming many years, we will count on the role of AI in justice to end up even greater profound. AI's ability to system sizable quantities of statistics at speeds a ways beyond human talents offers the potential for greater accurate, constant, and green legal choices. It can help streamline legal approaches, lessen backlogs, and ensure that assets are dispensed greater pretty, in particular in overburdened legal structures.

However, as AI is integrated into justice systems, one of the most urgent demanding situations might be making sure that those structures are honest and loose from bias. AI algorithms are simplest as independent as the facts they are skilled on. If AI structures are trained on historic legal statistics that contains biases—including racial, gender, or socioeconomic bias—the algorithms may want to perpetuate and even exacerbate those biases. For example, an AI system utilized in sentencing tips may also propose harsher penalties for positive racial or ethnic organizations if it has been educated on biased data from a machine that has historically been discriminatory. The use of AI in such essential choices ought to undermine public agree with in the justice device and lead to unjust consequences.

To prevent bias in AI-based criminal structures, it's far critical to make sure that the records used to educate these algorithms is consultant, numerous, and loose from discrimination. Moreover, transparency in AI choice-making approaches will be crucial for holding systems accountable and ensuring fairness. Just as human judges are predicted to explain the rationale behind their selections, AI structures ought to be required to provide clear, comprehensible motives for the effects they produce. This will allow individuals to task choices and attraction while necessary, ensuring that the legal device remains simply and accountable.

The question of accountability additionally becomes more complex when AI is concerned in selection-making techniques. If an AI device makes a mistake or promises an unjust final results, who's accountable? Is it the developer of the AI, the prison group that deployed it, or the AI itself? In the absence of clear duty frameworks, the use of AI in the justice device may want to result in conditions in which people are wronged with out recourse, undermining the ideas of justice and fairness. Establishing clean legal frameworks that define responsibility and responsibility within the use of AI is crucial to make sure that justice is served, even if decisions are made by means of machines.

Another important aspect of the destiny of justice with AI is the capability for improved get right of entry to to felony offerings. AI has the potential to democratize legal offerings by making them extra less expensive and on hand to folks who won't otherwise be able to have the funds for representation. AI-driven equipment, along with chatbots, prison recommendation systems, and file era services, can offer low-fee, available felony assistance to human beings from all walks of life. In many regions, AI-powered platforms have already been used to help human beings recognize their prison rights, draft contracts, and navigate complicated criminal approaches. These tools have the ability to revolutionize get admission to to justice, in particular in underserved groups in which legal services are scarce or prohibitively luxurious.

Additionally, AI can assist in improving the efficiency and equity of dispute decision mechanisms. AI-powered arbitration and mediation systems ought to offer faster, much less pricey, and more neutral options to conventional litigation, lowering the burden on courts and permitting events to solve their disputes greater successfully. These systems, however, might want to be cautiously designed to make sure they may be free from bias, transparent, and able to don't forget the nuances of every person case. As the use of AI in dispute resolution grows, it will likely be vital to balance efficiency with the want for human judgment, empathy, and understanding.

The function of AI in restorative justice is some other area that might see great improvement inside the future. Restorative justice specializes in repairing harm and restoring relationships, in place of absolutely punishing offenders. AI could be used to research records and offer insights that help pick out underlying causes of crime, which include socioeconomic elements, intellectual health troubles, or systemic inequality. By integrating AI with restorative justice practices, there may be potential to create a more holistic approach to justice that now not best punishes offenders but additionally addresses the basis causes of crime and helps restoration for both sufferers and offenders.

However, the destiny of justice with AI isn't always without its ethical dilemmas. One of the important thing problems that ought to be addressed is the stability between technological advancement and human rights. The growing use of AI in surveillance, predictive policing, and monitoring raises concerns about privacy, civil liberties, and the capacity for authoritarian manage. The integration of AI into the justice machine ought to be accomplished in a way that respects man or woman rights, ensures fairness, and stops the overreach of kingdom electricity. For example, whilst AI ought to help expect and prevent crime, it's far crucial to save you its misuse in approaches that disproportionately target certain groups or violate individuals' proper to privacy.

Furthermore, as AI structures turn out to be extra sophisticated, the query of whether AI ought to have a function in judicial selection-making will become greater complex. Should machines have the authority to make final selections in criminal topics, or must they stay equipment that assist human judges and criminal experts? Many argue that the human element in justice—empathy, intuition, and an know-how of ethical values—is irreplaceable. While AI can offer precious insights, the ultimate duty for criminal choices may also need to stay within the hands of humans to make certain that justice isn't always only served but gave the impression to be served.

In end, the future of justice with AI is full of both huge promise and sizable demanding situations. AI has the capability to improve the performance, accessibility, and equity of felony structures, however handiest if it's miles evolved and implemented in a manner that prioritizes fairness, transparency, and human rights. As AI continues to reshape the prison panorama, it will likely be important to create frameworks that cope with the moral, criminal, and social implications of its use in justice. By carefully balancing the advantages of AI with a commitment to shielding essential human values, we are able to ensure that the destiny of justice stays honest, equitable, and aligned with the needs of society.

4.4. AI and Access to Opportunities

Artificial intelligence (AI) is increasingly more shaping the panorama of opportunity throughout more than one sectors consisting of training, employment, finance, healthcare, and beyond. Its transformative potential promises to democratize get entry to, personalize services, and free up new pathways for social and economic advancement. However, AI's position in increasing or constraining get right of entry to to opportunities is complicated and double-edged. While AI structures can reduce traditional limitations and enlarge person capabilities, in addition they hazard perpetuating or even exacerbating existing inequalities if no longer thoughtfully designed and ruled. This chapter explores how AI influences access to possibilities, the mechanisms through which it operates, and the ethical, social, and coverage considerations essential to make certain that AI fosters inclusion in preference to exclusion.

One of the most seen methods AI affects get right of entry to is thru its integration into recruitment and hiring strategies. Automated resume screening, predictive analytics, and candidate ranking algorithms promise to streamline selection and reduce human bias. These systems can speedy parse large volumes of programs, discover qualified applicants, and suit capabilities to task necessities with remarkable performance. For candidates from underrepresented or marginalized organizations, AI holds the potential to level the playing area by using focusing on goal standards and skill-primarily based checks. However, in exercise, those structures often reflect and make stronger historic biases embedded in education statistics. For example, if beyond hiring selections disproportionately preferred sure demographics, the AI may additionally discover ways to mirror the ones patterns, systematically disadvantaging others. This phenomenon can restrict access to process possibilities for girls, minorities, and non-traditional candidates, thereby entrenching inequalities as opposed to mitigating them.

In schooling, AI-pushed adaptive mastering structures customize education by means of dynamically adjusting content material and pacing according to a learner's desires. Such technology can provide college students from numerous backgrounds with tailor-made aid, allowing better engagement and improved results. Furthermore, AI can amplify access to satisfactory education in far off or underserved areas via online tutoring, language translation, and automated grading. These improvements preserve promise for democratizing schooling globally. Yet demanding situations continue to be. Unequal get right of entry to to digital infrastructure, disparities in information high-quality, and the danger of algorithmic bias may additionally preclude equitable blessings. Moreover, reliance on AI may additionally inadvertently marginalize beginners who do not healthy wellknown studying models or who require human mentorship past what AI can offer. Ensuring that AI enhances as opposed to replaces human educators is essential for equitable possibility.

Finance is some other quarter in which AI reshapes access to opportunity. Credit scoring algorithms powered through AI compare loan packages with more velocity and precision, potentially expanding credit get admission to to those formerly excluded due to loss of conventional credit records. AI-driven microfinance platforms and digital banking offerings have added monetary inclusion to tens of millions globally. Nevertheless, the opacity of a few AI models raises issues approximately equity and discrimination. Factors correlated with covered characteristics, which includes area or employment type, may be unfairly weighted, ensuing in biased lending choices. Furthermore, algorithmic choices may also lack transparency, leaving applicants not able to understand or contest denials. Policies promoting explainability, equity audits, and person recourse are vital to ensure AI enables as opposed to restricts economic possibilities.

Healthcare get admission to has also been transformed by AI, from diagnostic guide systems to personalised treatment pointers. AI can pick out patterns in clinical data to locate diseases earlier and extra appropriately than some traditional strategies, improving preventive care and treatment consequences. Remote diagnostics and telemedicine powered with the aid of AI extend healthcare access to rural and underserved populations. Yet disparities in education data reflecting underrepresented organizations chance misdiagnosis or inadequate care for minorities. Moreover, the digital divide may additionally restrict access to AI-enabled healthcare innovations for economically disadvantaged sufferers. Ethical deployment requires making sure numerous datasets, culturally in a position algorithms, and infrastructural investment to bridge get admission to gaps.

Beyond these sectors, AI affects get right of entry to to opportunities in social offerings, prison aid, housing, or even innovative industries. Automated eligibility assessments for social welfare applications can streamline aid but can also exclude prone people because of flawed information or inflexible standards. AI in prison analytics can improve get admission to to justice through supporting in case research and record evaluation, yet might also improve concerns about equity if choice-help gear are used with out right human oversight. In innovative domain names, AI-generated content and tools can decrease access obstacles, enabling broader participation in artwork, song, and literature, although questions on intellectual assets and authenticity emerge.

Crucially, AI's effect on possibility is formed by means of the records it learns from. Historical and structural inequalities embedded in statistics reflect systemic discrimination and social stratification. If AI systems are skilled without interest to those biases, they risk perpetuating exclusion and injustice. Addressing this requires proactive bias detection, various facts sourcing, and continuous tracking. Inclusive layout procedures that engage stakeholders from marginalized communities assist make sure that AI programs reflect numerous stories and desires.

Governance and law play a pivotal position in shaping equitable get right of entry to to opportunities mediated through AI. Legal frameworks that enforce non-discrimination, mandate transparency, and require impact exams help safeguard against harmful consequences. Standards for statistics ethics, privateness, and algorithmic accountability sell accept as true with and equity. Public and private quarter collaboration is essential to increase tips that stability innovation with safety of susceptible organizations.

Educational tasks are also essential to democratize AI benefits. Digital literacy packages empower people to recognize, question, and leverage AI technology. Workforce reskilling and lifelong mastering initiatives put together populations for AI-driven labor marketplace transformations, decreasing the threat of technological displacement. Efforts to diversify AI research and improvement groups decorate cultural competence and ethical sensitivity, fostering structures that serve broader constituencies.

AI holds transformative capability to increase access to possibilities, lessen obstacles, and empower people throughout socioeconomic spectra. Yet understanding this capability demands deliberate attention to the socio-technical dynamics shaping AI's deployment. Addressing data biases, ensuring transparency, fostering inclusive layout, and enacting robust governance are imperative to save you AI from turning into a new vector of exclusion. As societies an increasing number of rely upon AI to allocate opportunities, the task lies now not best in technological innovation however in embedding equity, justice, and human dignity on the heart of AI structures. Through those efforts, AI can come to be a tool for empowerment in place of marginalization, opening new horizons of opportunity for all.

4.5. Algorithmic Fairness in Public Services

As synthetic intelligence increasingly more integrates into the fabric of public services, the precept of algorithmic equity emerges as a important concern with profound societal implications. Governments and public establishments rent AI-pushed systems to make choices in areas such as welfare distribution, criminal justice, healthcare allocation, training, and public protection. While those programs promise stronger efficiency, consistency, and scalability, additionally they threat perpetuating or amplifying current social inequities if fairness isn't always carefully ensured. Algorithmic equity in public services is as a consequence now not simply a technical mission but a democratic imperative, worrying a complete method that intertwines ethical concepts, prison frameworks, technical rigor, and public responsibility.

Public services range essentially from many non-public zone programs due to the fact they without delay effect citizens' rights, opportunities, and properly-being, regularly under the aegis of the social agreement. Consequently, the fairness of algorithms utilized in these domain names is paramount to preserving public agree with and upholding standards of equality and justice. For example, risk assessment equipment inside the criminal justice device, which expect recidivism quotes to tell parole selections, have come under scrutiny for embedding racial biases that disproportionately affect minority populations. Similarly, AI algorithms deployed for social welfare eligibility dedication may additionally inadvertently exclude inclined individuals due to incomplete or biased statistics. These instances highlight the tangible effects of unfair algorithms and underscore the necessity for transparent, equitable AI governance in public sectors.

Defining fairness itself is a complex undertaking, complicated through the plurality of normative views and technical interpretations. Different formal fairness metrics exist—along with demographic parity, same opportunity, and predictive parity—every prioritizing exclusive notions of equity and statistical stability. However, enjoyable all fairness criteria concurrently is mathematically impossible in lots of real-world situations, main to exchange-offs that require value judgments knowledgeable by way of social context and coverage dreams. Hence, selections approximately which fairness definitions to adopt need to contain stakeholders beyond technologists, which includes ethicists, criminal professionals, affected groups, and policymakers.

Achieving algorithmic equity begins with cautious attention to facts. Public service datasets often mirror ancient injustices, systemic discrimination, and socio-economic disparities. Without correction, education AI fashions on such records dangers encoding bias into automated selection-making. Data curation efforts, consisting of bias detection, balancing, and augmentation, are necessary but insufficient on their personal. Developers must put into effect equity-conscious machine studying techniques that adjust model training goals to mitigate discriminatory consequences. Examples encompass reweighting samples, incorporating equity constraints, and using hostile de-biasing tactics. However, those technical interventions ought to be contextualized inside the public carrier's undertaking and prison duties.

Transparency and explainability are essential enhances to equity. Public believe hinges at the ability to understand how AI structures operate and make choices. Explainable AI (XAI) strategies can provide insights into characteristic significance, decision pathways, and model barriers, allowing oversight bodies and affected individuals to assess equity claims seriously. Moreover, transparency facilitates auditing and responsibility, allowing regulators and civil society to locate and address unfair practices proactively.

Governance frameworks play a important role in embedding fairness into public zone AI. Legal mandates consisting of the European Union's General Data Protection Regulation (GDPR) put into effect rights associated with automatic choice-making, together with transparency, contestability, and non-discrimination. Emerging guidelines precise to AI more and more emphasize fairness as a core requirement. Beyond felony compliance, many governments set up ethical pointers, independent oversight bodies, and participatory mechanisms to involve citizens in AI policy formation. These institutional structures assist make sure that AI deployment aligns with societal values and human rights.

Public area groups must also domesticate an internal tradition that prioritizes fairness. This entails schooling AI practitioners and selection-makers in ethical concerns, establishing interdisciplinary groups such as social scientists and ethicists, and integrating fairness checks into development workflows. Continuous tracking of deployed structures is important to stumble on shifts in records distributions or performance disparities through the years. Feedback loops that contain consumer reports and proceedings beautify responsiveness and corrective motion.

Furthermore, fairness in public services should recall intersectionality—the way wherein overlapping social identities together with race, gender, elegance, and disability compound stories of discrimination. Algorithms which can be truthful when evaluated on a single attribute may additionally nevertheless produce unjust consequences for corporations on the intersection of multiple marginalized identities. Addressing this complexity requires sophisticated fairness metrics and multidimensional analyses, as well as engagement with the lived experiences of various groups.

Finally, algorithmic equity intersects with broader societal efforts to address structural inequities. While honest AI can mitigate a few harms, it cannot alternative for complete social rules geared toward reducing poverty, systemic racism, and unequal get right of entry to to resources. AI equity should be part of an integrated method that consists of training, monetary opportunity, and social justice tasks.

Ensuring algorithmic fairness in public offerings is a multifaceted undertaking that needs technological innovation, moral mirrored image, legal oversight, and democratic participation. As AI structures increasingly form public selection-making, embedding equity safeguards is crucial to guard character rights, preserve social cohesion, and promote equitable effects. By confronting these challenges head-on, societies can harness the advantages of AI while honoring the fundamental values that underpin public service.

CHAPTER 5

AI and the Moral Dilemma

5.1. AI's Confrontation with Moral Dilemmas

As artificial intelligence (AI) keeps to advance, one of the maximum urgent demanding situations we face is the moral dilemmas AI structures can also stumble upon. These dilemmas venture no longer simplest the programming of machines but additionally the very ethics of decision-making in contexts wherein human lives, values, and rights are at stake.

AI systems are not inherently ethical or immoral; they're equipment constructed by way of people with the ability to method huge quantities of records, pick out patterns, and make selections primarily based on algorithms. However, as AI structures come to be greater autonomous, they're confronted with conditions in which there are no smooth solutions. These conditions often contain conflicting moral concepts, where choices made by way of AI ought to have vast moral implications.

The most classic instance of AI confronting a moral dilemma comes from the area of autonomous motors. Imagine a self-riding vehicle faced with a surprising impediment on the road. It should make a split-second selection: Should it steer to hit one person, thereby saving the others in the car, or should it avoid the obstacle, doubtlessly endangering the lives of its occupants but saving the ones outdoor the vehicle? This scenario encapsulates the traditional "trolley problem," a moral notion experiment that has been extensively discussed within the context of AI ethics. The trouble is a complicated one, because it forces us to confront essential questions on utilitarianism, rights, and the value of human existence.

Autonomous automobiles, healthcare structures, army drones, and AI in social policy all contain conditions in which AI ought to make selections that impact human well-being. In healthcare, as an instance, an AI might be tasked with recommending treatments for patients, however it may face a quandary where one remedy is extra effective for one institution of sufferers but poses big dangers to any other. AI's decision-making in those contexts turns into specially fraught while considering the human elements of bias, privateness, and fairness.

The middle of the ethical quandary faced by using AI lies inside the reality that it's far frequently now not geared up to understand the nuances of human emotions, relationships, and cultural values. While an AI machine might be capable to investigate records and are expecting results with exceptional precision, it can't feel empathy or hold close the emotional weight of its decisions. This highlights the important anxiety between the objective nature of algorithms and the subjective reviews that regularly inform moral selections.

Moreover, AI's decision-making is most effective as suitable as the information it's far trained on. If the facts it methods carries biases, those biases will necessarily be pondered in its selections. This creates a moral dilemma due to the fact an AI gadget may want to perpetuate inequalities or discriminate towards certain corporations with none human intention. Addressing those biases is critical to making sure that AI does now not by chance purpose harm or uphold societal inequalities, however it additionally affords a project in how we make sure fairness in gadget gaining knowledge of algorithms.

As AI structures are integrated into increasingly complicated sectors of society, the ethical dilemmas they face are probable to develop. The assignment is not handiest about ensuring that AI structures make choices that align with our moral values, however also approximately determining who is responsible while AI systems make harmful or unethical choices. Should the creators of these structures be held accountable? Or must the AI itself bear responsibility for its actions, in particular in cases of accidental harm?

These questions of accountability and moral organization deliver us to the fundamental problem of AI's function in society. Should AI be considered merely as a tool that supports human selection-making, or should it's identified as an independent entity able to making moral choices? This philosophical question stays a subject of extreme debate, particularly as AI structures grow to be extra superior and able to making choices that have far-accomplishing effects.

The confrontation among AI and moral dilemmas increases profound questions about the destiny of era and ethics. As AI systems keep to conform, we must grapple with how we want machines to navigate complicated moral landscapes and the way we, as a society, can ensure that AI's choices are aligned with our collective ethical standards. This ongoing dialogue will form the function of AI in our lives and decide the moral framework within which these technology perform.

5.2. AI and Human Security

As artificial intelligence (AI) structures grow to be more and more incorporated into diverse sectors, one of the critical issues is their effect on human protection. This trouble encompasses both bodily and digital nation-states, in which AI's involvement can gift dangers in addition to possibilities for shielding people, societies, and nations. The intersection of AI and human protection increases critical questions about the way to make sure that AI systems guard, instead of threaten, human properly-being in all contexts.

AI's capability to decorate human security is full-size. In fields like healthcare, law enforcement, protection, and disaster reaction, AI technologies offer remarkable capabilities to expect, save you, and mitigate threats. For instance, in public protection, AI-driven surveillance systems can examine big quantities of information to come across ability criminal pastime or pick out emerging threats, doubtlessly preventing harm earlier than it occurs. Similarly, AI's position in cybersecurity, in which it's miles employed to come across and respond to malicious interest in actual-time, is pivotal in protecting in opposition to a growing variety of cyber threats.

In healthcare, AI is also located to enhance protection by means of enhancing diagnostics, treatment accuracy, and the efficiency of emergency responses. For instance, AI-powered structures can pick out patterns in clinical information that might move overlooked by means of human practitioners, enabling earlier detection of diseases, and in the end improving affected person consequences. AI's capability to expect and model potential disease outbreaks or public fitness crises is any other location wherein it can safeguard human protection on a international scale.

Despite these advantages, the rise of AI presents substantial dangers to human protection, specifically when AI structures are misused, poorly designed, or malfunction. One of the most immediate concerns is the weaponization of AI. Autonomous drones, independent weapons systems, and AI-driven navy technologies have the potential to alter the panorama of battle, creating new risks to each combatants and civilians. The ability for AI to make choices in lifestyles-and-loss of life conditions without human oversight raises profound ethical and security issues, especially when it comes to issues of duty and the capacity for unintended escalation in struggle zones.

AI systems, because of their complexity, also are susceptible to hacking and manipulation. A compromised AI system might be hijacked to wreak havoc on vital infrastructure, from energy grids to transportation systems, doubtlessly endangering millions of lives. Such assaults ought to result in the disruption of crucial offerings, compromising human safety and stability in affected areas. The vulnerability of AI systems to cyberattacks underscores the significance of cybersecurity in safeguarding human safety. As AI structures become more familiar in crucial sectors like electricity, verbal exchange, and transportation, their resilience to attacks becomes crucial for maintaining societal properly-being.

In the digital realm, AI's role in surveillance and information collection additionally raises questions about privateness and civil liberties. While AI can enhance protection with the aid of monitoring for threats, it may also infringe upon people' rights if misused. In authoritarian regimes, as an instance, AI-enabled surveillance can be used to screen and suppress dissent, posing a hazard to non-public freedoms and societal stability. Ensuring that AI's use in surveillance is moral and transparent, with appropriate safeguards in place to defend privacy, is vital in balancing the want for protection with the protection of person rights.

AI's potential for selection-making, while applied to high-stakes situations consisting of emergency response, also can pose demanding situations. In disaster situations, AI can be deployed to triage patients, allocate resources, or control evacuation efforts. However, the reliance on AI structures to make decisions that effect human lives increases concerns about equity, transparency, and responsibility. If an AI system have been to make an wrong or biased choice, it may have life-altering effects, similarly complicating efforts to ensure the safety of susceptible populations.

Furthermore, AI's developing role in non-public gadgets and smart technology has delivered new dangers to human safety. From voice-activated assistants to self-driving motors, AI-driven gadgets are constantly gathering records about people' actions, possibilities, and conduct. While this statistics can enhance person studies and enhance protection, it also creates new vulnerabilities. Personal facts will be exploited for malicious purposes, together with identity theft, or used to manipulate conduct thru focused incorrect information campaigns. As people end up increasingly dependent on AI structures for every day activities, shielding this facts from breaches or misuse is vital to maintaining private security.

AI's capability to beautify safety need to also be weighed towards the potential for creating new forms of inequality. Access to AI-powered security technology may want to disproportionately advantage positive agencies, leaving others greater vulnerable to protection threats. For instance, superior surveillance structures may be used predominantly in wealthier or extra evolved regions, leaving marginalized groups less covered. Similarly, the uneven distribution of AI's advantages in healthcare or schooling should exacerbate present disparities in access to essential services, undermining efforts to promote worldwide human safety.

Addressing these risks requires a multifaceted method that entails governments, industries, and global agencies. Developing global frameworks for the responsible use of AI, ensuring transparency in AI's layout and implementation, and maintaining AI structures responsible for their movements are key to ensuring that AI contributes positively to human security. Moreover, embedding ethical considerations into the improvement of AI technologies is critical for stopping misuse and minimizing the capacity for damage.

AI's role in human safety gives both widespread possibilities and challenges. As AI keeps to adapt, it's far important that we expand strategies to harness its potential while addressing the dangers it poses. The destiny of human safety will rely now not handiest on technological improvements however additionally on how correctly we navigate the ethical, political, and societal problems that accompany the upward push of AI. By drawing close AI with a dedication to safeguarding human dignity, privacy, and rights, we can make certain that AI serves as a force for right, enhancing protection at the same time as minimizing damage.

5.3. The Role of AI in Society

The growing presence of synthetic intelligence (AI) in society marks a transformative shift in the way individuals, groups, and establishments characteristic. AI has already established its capability to reshape numerous sectors, from healthcare to transportation, schooling to entertainment, and even governance. However, the deeper implications of AI's position in society extend beyond its technological capabilities, raising essential questions about its have an effect on on social systems, relationships, and cultural norms.

At the middle of AI's societal function is its ability to drive exceptional ranges of performance and innovation. In the enterprise global, AI structures allow groups to automate methods, enhance customer service, and beautify choice-making abilities. AI's potential to investigate huge datasets quick and as it should be allows for the development of greater powerful strategies and solutions. As industries maintain to adopt AI, the capability for economic growth and productivity increases, however so does the risk of significant disruption. Jobs in traditional sectors can be changed by way of automation, main to a change within the exertions marketplace and requiring a reevaluation of body of workers structures.

While AI has the ability to reinforce productiveness, it also increases concerns approximately unemployment and income inequality. The automation of habitual responsibilities in industries which include production, transportation, and retail threatens to displace millions of people, especially those in low-talent jobs. Although AI can create new opportunities in tech-centric fields, the transition won't be smooth for those whose abilities are not at once transferable to the AI-driven economic system. As a result, society faces the mission of ensuring that employees displaced by using AI technologies are furnished with opportunities for retraining and skill improvement to remain relevant in an evolving task market.

The societal effect of AI extends to the area of privateness and personal freedoms. AI systems are increasingly more embedded in ordinary existence, from smart gadgets to surveillance networks. These technology have the capability to enhance comfort and decorate security, but they also increase huge worries approximately the erosion of privacy. The big quantity of private information accumulated by means of AI systems may be exploited for business benefit, probably compromising people' private records and autonomy. Additionally, the usage of AI in surveillance, whether or not by using governments or non-public companies, raises moral questions about the balance between security and privateness. The ongoing debate over records ownership, consent, and surveillance practices is primary to information AI's position in shaping societal norms and values.

Furthermore, AI's integration into governance and regulation enforcement introduces new demanding situations concerning accountability, bias, and fairness. AI systems utilized in crook justice, for example, have the potential to streamline operations and boom performance. However, these systems are not proof against biases, and their use in decision-making techniques can perpetuate present inequalities. Predictive policing algorithms, as an example, might also disproportionately goal minority communities, reinforcing societal divisions. Ensuring that AI technology are deployed equitably and transparently is important in stopping discrimination and fostering consider in AI-pushed structures.

The function of AI in shaping social interactions is every other vital factor of its have an impact on on society. Social media structures, powered via AI algorithms, have an effect on the statistics people are uncovered to, shaping public opinion and political discourse. While AI-pushed content material recommendation structures have the capability to curate personalized stories, they also raise concerns about the unfold of misinformation and the amplification of echo chambers. The ease with which AI can generate and distribute content online gives new risks for manipulation, from deepfakes to fake news, undermining consider in records sources. The project for society is to make sure that AI's have an effect on on public discourse is controlled in a manner that promotes the loose drift of accurate records whilst curtailing the spread of harmful content.

AI's effect on social cohesion extends to the world of healthcare, education, and social services. In healthcare, AI technology allow greater accurate diagnoses, personalized treatment plans, and better access to hospital treatment. AI-powered gear can examine scientific data to pick out styles and are expecting results, helping doctors make informed decisions. While AI's contributions to healthcare are in large part superb, demanding situations remain in making sure that access to these technology is equitable, particularly in underserved or marginalized communities. The adoption of AI in healthcare could exacerbate existing disparities if now not cautiously controlled, leaving vulnerable populations with limited get entry to to superior care.

Similarly, AI's role in schooling holds promise for personalised learning and advanced educational consequences. AI-pushed systems can assess students' development, pick out regions for improvement, and tailor classes to individual desires. While those innovations have the capability to transform training, additionally they raise worries approximately the standardization of learning reports and the reinforcement of biases in algorithmic models. Ensuring that AI in education is designed to decorate range and inclusion, instead of reinforcing present inequalities, is fundamental to ensuring that its impact on students is fine.

The cultural implications of AI's function in society also are profound. As AI systems end up more advanced, they task traditional notions of creativity, authorship, and human ingenuity. In fields inclusive of artwork, song, and literature, AI-generated works are already pushing the boundaries of creativity. However, the question arises: who owns the rights to AI-generated works? Can a machine be considered an artist, or is creativity inherently human? The debate surrounding AI's position inside the innovative industries raises complicated questions about intellectual property, originality, and the character of creative expression. As AI maintains to play a larger function in cultural production, society have to grapple with these questions and redefine its know-how of creativity.

In addition to its cultural impact, AI's societal role is intertwined with broader moral considerations. As AI structures benefit autonomy, the difficulty of accountability turns into increasingly important. Who is responsible while an AI machine makes a selection that harms people or society? Should the creators, customers, or the AI machine itself be held responsible? These questions are crucial to making sure that AI's integration into society is achieved in a accountable and moral way. The development of frameworks for AI duty and governance is vital for retaining consider in AI systems and making sure that their deployment aligns with societal values and ideas.

AI's role in society will hold to adapt as technologies enhance and their packages expand. The demanding situations it provides are multifaceted, requiring careful thought and attention at each degree of development and deployment. From making sure fairness in AI's advantages to handling its impact on privateness, employment, and social cohesion, society ought to take an energetic role in shaping AI's destiny. By fostering dialogue, growing moral guidelines, and prioritizing human-focused values, we can navigate the complexities of AI's position in society and work toward a destiny in which its benefits are broadly shared, and its dangers are efficaciously managed.

5.4. Navigating AI's Dual-Use Potential

Artificial intelligence stands at the crossroads of remarkable possibility and complicated chance. Its twin-use nature—where the identical technology can be harnessed for both beneficial and harmful purposes—poses a powerful undertaking for developers, policymakers, and society at large. On one hand, AI offers transformative answers across healthcare, environmental monitoring, training, and enterprise. On the opposite, it can be weaponized, misused for surveillance and manage, or inadvertently motive damage via accidental results. Navigating AI's twin-use potential calls for a nuanced understanding of its capabilities, vigilant governance, moral foresight, and collaborative worldwide frameworks to maximize benefits at the same time as mitigating risks.

The idea of dual-use era isn't new; nuclear power, biotechnology, and cryptography have long embodied this paradox. However, AI's speedy evolution and broad applicability enlarge the stakes. For instance, gadget learning algorithms that enable breakthroughs in clinical diagnostics can also be repurposed for developing self sustaining weapons or state-of-the-art cyberattacks. Deepfake technologies that democratize content material creation and artwork can simultaneously facilitate misinformation, fraud, and political manipulation. Autonomous structures designed for logistics and transportation can be adapted for navy drones or surveillance devices. This duality complicates efforts to govern AI development and deployment without stifling innovation.

One center assignment lies in the problem of honestly distinguishing benign from malicious AI packages. Unlike conventional weapons, AI is software program-based and regularly constructed on open-source structures reachable globally. Its components—algorithms, datasets, computing electricity—can be combined and modified swiftly. This flexibility makes export controls and regulatory measures complex to design and implement. Moreover, the tempo of AI research and deployment outstrips the velocity of policymaking, creating regulatory gaps that awful actors may additionally exploit. Consequently, governance strategies should stability security concerns with openness and innovation, averting overly restrictive guidelines that prevent beneficial uses.

Ethical frameworks emphasize the obligation of AI researchers and organizations to assume twin-use risks during the layout and improvement stages. Principles which includes "accountable innovation" and "precautionary methods" suggest for embedding safety, transparency, and human oversight mechanisms to prevent misuse. For instance, developers can implement get entry to controls, monitoring systems, and utilization restrictions for touchy AI models. Differential privateness and federated getting to know techniques shield facts confidentiality, lowering the risk of exploitation. Ethical overview forums and internal governance systems can examine tasks for capacity dual-use consequences, fostering a lifestyle of conscientious AI development.

At the policy level, global cooperation is essential. AI's without boundaries nature needs collaborative frameworks similar to nuclear non-proliferation or biological weapons treaties. Multilateral establishments, which include the United Nations, the OECD, and specialised AI governance our bodies, play critical roles in fostering talk, putting norms, and coordinating oversight. Shared requirements on transparency, safety, and ethics can harmonize efforts across international locations, minimizing dangers of AI arms races or misuse. Yet geopolitical rivalries and divergent countrywide hobbies complicate consensus-building, underscoring the want for consider-building measures and inclusive participation.

Dual-use AI demanding situations additionally name for robust detection and reaction abilties. Cybersecurity infrastructures must evolve to perceive and mitigate AI-pushed threats which includes computerized hacking, records poisoning, or incorrect information campaigns. Governments and private sectors must put money into threat intelligence sharing, rapid response teams, and AI-powered defense tools. Simultaneously, transparency and public consciousness campaigns can empower customers to recognize and resist malicious AI-generated content material or manipulations.

Another measurement is the socio-political impact of dual-use AI. Surveillance technology powered by facial recognition and conduct evaluation, while deployed under authoritarian regimes, might also suppress dissent and violate human rights. On the flip facet, these gear can enhance public safety and law enforcement effectiveness in democratic societies if well regulated. Balancing protection blessings with civil liberties requires sturdy prison safeguards, oversight, and mechanisms for redress.

Research into AI safety and alignment addresses lengthy-term dual-use worries. Ensuring that increasingly independent

AI systems act according with human values and intentions is paramount to save you catastrophic misuse or injuries. This includes growing interpretability methods, fail-safe architectures, and fee alignment techniques. Investments in AI protection studies, supported by using public and personal sectors, help anticipate and mitigate existential risks associated with superior AI competencies.

The private area plays a vital function in navigating twin-use challenges. Technology agencies, startups, and research institutions wield big have an impact on over AI trajectories. Industry self-law, moral tips, and collaborative initiatives like the Partnership on AI reveal efforts to manipulate twin-use dangers responsibly. However, industrial pressures and aggressive dynamics every now and then struggle with warning, necessitating obvious reporting, stakeholder engagement, and outside accountability mechanisms.

Navigating AI's dual-use ability demands an integrated technique combining moral foresight, technical safeguards, policy innovation, global cooperation, and public engagement. The goal is not to halt AI development but to steer it in the direction of beneficial ends even as proactively dealing with risks. Success depends on recognizing the inseparable nature of opportunity and peril in AI technology and committing to shared stewardship that protects humanity's collective future. Through vigilance, collaboration, and principled movement, society can harness AI's promise whilst safeguarding in opposition to its misuse.

5.5. AI and the Future of Human Values

As artificial intelligence systems turn out to be increasingly more embedded within the cloth of regular lifestyles, the query of ways AI will form—and be formed by using—human values is each pressing and profound. Human values encompass a vast spectrum of ethical principles, cultural norms, emotional sensibilities, and social priorities that outline societies and people. The interplay between AI and these values is not unidirectional; alternatively, it is a dynamic, evolving relationship in which AI technologies impact human behaviors and decisions, whilst human values guide the design, deployment, and law of AI. Understanding this complex interplay is crucial to ensuring that AI development aligns with the collective aspirations of humanity and fosters a destiny wherein era complements in place of erodes our center values.

At the coronary heart of this discourse lies the recognition that AI systems do not own intrinsic values or focus; their conduct reflects the targets, facts, and layout alternatives instilled by means of human creators. Yet, as AI increasingly participates in choice-making—starting from healthcare guidelines to judicial exams, from social media content curation to self reliant automobiles—its affect on social norms, man or woman autonomy, and cultural practices intensifies. This increases important questions: Which human values should AI prioritize? How can various and sometimes conflicting values be encoded into algorithms? And how will the huge adoption of AI reshape collective understandings of justice, privacy, empathy, and identity?

One of the number one issues is cost alignment: the venture of making sure that AI systems perform constantly with human values. Misalignment risks producing consequences which are harmful, unjust, or alien to societal expectations. For instance, AI optimizing solely for performance in healthcare aid allocation may additionally forget about fairness and compassion, disproportionately disadvantaging inclined populations. Researchers are growing frameworks and methodologies to encode values explicitly into AI systems, through techniques which include ethical constraint programming, desire mastering, and participatory design strategies that include stakeholder input. However, fee pluralism—where exclusive cultures or people preserve divergent values—makes generic alignment complex, necessitating adaptable and context-touchy AI models.

Privacy represents a essential human fee increasingly challenged by using AI. Surveillance abilties powered by AI's information processing can erode person autonomy and anonymity, doubtlessly undermining consider in institutions and interpersonal relationships. The future of privacy in an AI-enabled international depends on how societies negotiate trade-offs between protection, convenience, and confidentiality. Concepts such as "privacy by means of design" and sturdy information governance frameworks are searching for to embed recognize for privateness into AI systems from inception, reflecting a commitment to keeping human dignity amid technological develop.

Justice and fairness are center human values profoundly stricken by AI. The deployment of AI in law enforcement, credit score scoring, hiring, and social services highlights the risk of perpetuating systemic biases thru algorithmic selection-making. Ensuring that AI respects fairness includes now not simplest technical fixes—like bias mitigation and transparency—but also broader societal efforts to deal with structural inequalities. Moreover, AI's interpretability affects perceptions of justice: human beings call for explanations for selections that affect their lives, linking equity to duty and accept as true with.

The future of empathy and emotional connection additionally faces transformation through AI. Social robots, digital assistants, and affective computing systems are designed to recognize, simulate, or respond to human feelings. While those technology can provide companionship and assist, they enhance questions about authenticity and the character of human relationships. Will reliance on AI companions adjust social behaviors or lessen human-to-human empathy? Balancing technological facilitation of emotional nicely-being with maintenance of actual human interaction is a key ethical frontier.

AI's have an effect on on identification and autonomy introduces similarly complexity. Personalized algorithms form the information individuals consume, potentially reinforcing echo chambers and affecting self-perception. The capability of AI to generate artificial media demanding situations notions of reality and believe, with implications for cultural narratives and collective reminiscence. Moreover, AI's position in augmenting human talents—through brain-computer interfaces or cognitive enhancement—increases philosophical questions about the limits of human identity and business enterprise.

Governance and law play a pivotal role in embedding human values into AI's destiny. Ethical tips, legal frameworks, and standards have to replicate societal consensus whilst allowing flexibility for innovation and cultural range. Participatory methods concerning civil society, marginalized businesses, and interdisciplinary professionals help make sure that AI respects pluralistic values and mitigates dangers of exclusion or harm.

Education and public engagement are similarly critical to cultivate shared expertise and knowledgeable choice-making regarding AI's role in society. Empowering individuals with AI literacy allows important reflection at the era's advantages and demanding situations, fostering democratic manipulate over AI trajectories.

The destiny of human values in the age of AI is neither predetermined nor static. It will be shaped by ongoing dialogue, negotiation, and model among technologists, policymakers, and society at large. By deliberately integrating ethical mirrored image and cultural sensitivity into AI development, humanity can guide those powerful gear closer to improving dignity, justice, empathy, and freedom. In doing so, AI turns into not only a technological innovation, but a associate in the collective venture of human flourishing.

CHAPTER 6

AI and Human Rights

6.1. The Impact of AI on Human Rights

The upward push of Artificial Intelligence (AI) has ushered in a brand new technology of technological improvements that promise to revolutionize numerous factors of society. However, as these technologies continue to adapt, questions surrounding their impact on human rights have grow to be increasingly urgent. AI's capacity to reshape industries, governance, or even every day life increases complicated ethical, prison, and social demanding situations.

One of the most giant concerns concerning AI's effect on human rights is its impact on privateness. AI-powered technologies, especially within the shape of surveillance structures, statistics mining, and facial reputation, can compromise an individual's proper to privacy. The ability of AI to investigate good sized quantities of private statistics—regularly without specific consent—has sparked debates about the erosion of privacy in the virtual age. Governments and corporations have increasingly more applied AI gear for surveillance purposes, doubtlessly infringing on an person's proper to keep their non-public facts private.

The big implementation of AI surveillance structures, including facial popularity in public areas, has raised concerns approximately "digital panopticism." This refers to the idea that AI allows consistent surveillance of individuals, turning entire populations into topics of scrutiny. While proponents argue that these technology are essential for public protection and crime prevention, critics contend that they enable authoritarian governments and groups to exert control over residents in unprecedented ways.

The mission, then, lies in balancing the want for safety and comfort with the protection of fundamental human rights. As AI continues to expand, it is important that policies are installed area to make sure that privateness is not unduly sacrificed for the sake of performance or safety.

AI's affect on freedom of expression is some other place wherein human rights are at chance. Social media platforms, information shops, and even search engines are more and more the usage of AI to curate content material, advocate articles, and slight discussions. While these equipment can improve user revel in, additionally they have the ability to limit the variety of data and ideas accessible to the public.

AI-pushed content material moderation structures, for instance, can also inadvertently censor valid political discourse or stifle dissent. The algorithms utilized by these structures are often opaque and may be influenced via biases inherent of their layout. When AI structures flag or eliminate content material primarily based on vague criteria or without human oversight, individuals may be denied their right to freely express their evaluations, especially if the ones critiques venture prevailing political, cultural, or social norms.

Moreover, AI's ability to manipulate media through deepfakes and synthetic content material poses extra threats to the integrity of public discourse. Misinformation and disinformation campaigns fueled by AI-generated content material can disrupt elections, incite violence, or create confusion. In such instances, human rights related to freedom of expression and get admission to to accurate records can be seriously undermined.

To mitigate those risks, a cautious examination of how AI is used to control and shape data is needed. Ensuring that freedom of expression stays protected in an AI-driven international requires transparency, accountability, and a dedication to stopping the misuse of AI for censorship.

Another essential location wherein AI intersects with human rights is within the realm of equality and discrimination. AI systems are designed to learn from big datasets, however if those datasets are biased or unrepresentative, the resulting algorithms can perpetuate and even exacerbate current inequalities. For instance, facial recognition technology has been proven to have better errors charges for girls and those of shade, main to concerns that AI might be used to disproportionately target positive agencies.

In the context of hiring and employment, AI-pushed recruitment tools are increasingly used to display screen activity applicants. However, if those tools are skilled on biased facts that reflects historic inequalities in the group of workers, they will prefer positive demographic corporations over others. This may want to lead to systemic discrimination towards women, racial minorities, or different marginalized groups. Similarly, predictive policing algorithms, which rely on AI to forecast crime hotspots, can make stronger biases within the criminal justice device, disproportionately affecting people of coloration and coffee-income communities.

AI's role in perpetuating inequality raises essential questions on the moral duty of developers, organizations, and governments in making sure that AI structures are designed and deployed in ways that sell fairness and inclusion. As AI becomes extra incorporated into decision-making techniques, it is important that efforts are made to address bias in each the records used to educate these structures and the algorithms that power them.

AI additionally raises vast questions on character autonomy and personal freedom. As AI structures emerge as more and more capable of making choices on behalf of people—ranging from economic transactions to healthcare picks—there may be the capacity for those structures to exert undue affect over private selections. For instance, AI-powered recommendation algorithms on streaming systems, e-commerce websites, and social media can create "filter bubbles" that restriction exposure to diverse views, for that reason constraining personal freedom with the aid of shaping individuals' ideals and options.

Moreover, the growing reliance on AI to make vital decisions in healthcare, criminal justice, and welfare structures may want to undermine individuals' autonomy. If AI systems are used to determine eligibility for scientific remedies or social benefits, there is a hazard that people may be denied their rights primarily based on algorithmic choices that they do not absolutely recognize or manage.

In some instances, AI could also be used to manipulate individuals' selections through persuasive design, customized commercials, and other behavioral interventions. This "nudging" effect may intrude with an man or woman's potential to make unfastened, informed decisions, as AI structures leverage large amounts of personal facts to subtly affect their possibilities and movements.

To safeguard human rights, it's miles essential to ensure that AI structures are obvious, responsible, and designed with the autonomy of individuals in thoughts. Ethical frameworks should be advanced to make certain that AI is used to empower people rather than constrain their freedom of choice.

In reaction to the developing impact of AI on human rights, there has been a concerted attempt to establish moral and felony frameworks that could guide the development and deployment of AI technology. Organizations which includes the European Union and the United Nations have issued pointers and tips on the moral use of AI, with a focal point on protecting essential rights including privateness, equality, and freedom of expression.

However, those frameworks are nonetheless evolving, and there's ongoing debate about the high-quality approaches to adjust AI at the same time as fostering innovation. The speedy pace of technological advancement makes it tough for policymakers to keep up with the moral implications of AI, specially in regions like facial recognition, predictive policing, and self reliant weapons structures. As such, there's a need for worldwide collaboration to make certain that AI is advanced in a way that respects human rights and promotes the commonplace excellent.

Moreover, ethical concerns need to be included into the layout and improvement of AI systems from the outset, rather than being an afterthought. AI researchers, engineers, and policymakers need to paintings together to create technology that prioritize human rights and cope with the ability harms related to AI.

The impact of AI on human rights is a complex and multifaceted issue that requires cautious consideration from more than one perspectives. As AI maintains to shape our global, it's far crucial to make certain that its development and deployment recognize fundamental human rights which includes privateness, freedom of expression, equality, and autonomy. By fostering transparency, responsibility, and ethical design practices, we will create an AI-pushed destiny that upholds the values of human dignity and freedom. The task lies in navigating the sensitive stability between innovation and the protection of rights, ensuring that AI serves the not unusual suitable without undermining the middle concepts of human life.

6.2. AI and Social Order and Human Rights

The intersection of Artificial Intelligence (AI) and human rights within the context of social order is a subject that has attracted vast attention as AI structures become more and more embedded in the fabric of societal infrastructure. From regulation enforcement to healthcare, employment, and past, AI performs a function in shaping how people and communities have interaction within the frameworks of governance, equality, and justice. However, even as AI guarantees to result in efficiencies and advancements, it additionally increases extreme issues approximately its implications on human rights and the very structure of social order itself.

As AI technology develop, their integration into society offers challenges and opportunities. These technologies have the capability to decorate social order by way of improving protection, streamlining governance, and offering new tools for addressing worldwide challenges. However, AI also can undermine essential human rights, create new kinds of inequality, and exacerbate social divides if now not carefully regulated and ethically managed.

One of the maximum immediately concerns concerning AI and social order is its function in surveillance. AI technologies are increasingly more used in monitoring populations for the purposes of national security, law enforcement, and crime prevention. Surveillance tools, consisting of facial popularity software program, predictive policing structures, and records-pushed tracking systems, were followed by governments and companies round the arena. While proponents argue that these structures are useful for boosting public safety and order, critics argue that they arrive with large threats to human rights, especially privateness and freedom of expression.

Surveillance equipment powered via AI can cause the mass series of private data, regularly without the consent of the people being monitored. This can result in breaches of privateness, the chilling of free speech, or even the criminalization of behaviors that aren't sincerely unlawful. For example, AI-pushed facial recognition structures have been broadly criticized for his or her potential to tune individuals in actual-time with out their information or consent, regularly elevating concerns about authoritarian manage and social manipulation.

Additionally, AI structures used for predictive policing—which includes algorithms designed to discover crime hotspots or forecast crook behavior—are regularly based totally on historical statistics that reflects pre-current biases. These biases can cause disproportionate concentrated on of marginalized groups, perpetuating racial and socio-economic inequalities inside the criminal justice machine. AI's role in surveillance is, therefore, a double-edged sword: while it could decorate regulation enforcement's capability to preserve order, it is able to additionally infringe on person liberties and human rights, especially in relation to privateness and anti-discrimination protections.

Beyond surveillance, AI has more and more been applied within the realm of governance and civil liberties. Governments are adopting AI to streamline administrative strategies, automate selection-making, and improve public services. AI-powered structures are hired in areas together with immigration, welfare distribution, education, and social security, aiming to optimize efficiency and service transport. However, there's a developing issue about the capability for AI structures to infringe on civil liberties while utilized in governmental selection-making techniques.

AI's use in governance can result in the erosion of transparency and responsibility in selection-making. AI structures, especially the ones utilising machine studying and big records analytics, could make decisions which are hard for human beings to apprehend or undertaking. For instance, AI-primarily based systems used to determine eligibility for welfare benefits or social offerings may additionally make selections which are opaque to the people affected. This lack of transparency can depart individuals feeling powerless to task choices made by way of algorithms that have an effect on their lives.

Additionally, when AI is used in governance, it can fail to account for the diverse needs of people from distinct backgrounds, main to systemic bias and inequity. If AI systems are skilled on biased datasets, they can perpetuate discrimination in regions inclusive of housing, employment, and social offerings. This is particularly concerning in societies that already face tremendous disparities in get right of entry to to sources and opportunities. AI's capacity to perpetuate bias and inequality increases essential questions about its function in shaping honest and just governance.

The fast improvement and deployment of AI technology additionally gift demanding situations related to financial inequality. AI structures are increasingly more getting used to optimize production, reduce costs, and growth profits throughout numerous industries. While these technologies have the capacity to boost productivity and create new monetary opportunities, they also danger exacerbating current economic divides. Automation powered by using AI has the potential to replace big numbers of jobs, especially in sectors like manufacturing, retail, and customer support, leading to process displacement and economic lack of confidence for susceptible people.

In this context, AI may want to have profound implications for human rights, specially the right to paintings and the proper to an adequate fashionable of residing. The displacement of employees through AI-driven automation could cause unemployment, salary stagnation, and improved poverty for certain segments of the populace. This is mainly genuine for employees in low-talent, guide exertions jobs, who may additionally discover it tough to transition to new roles with out the requisite education or training. In flip, the growing wealth generated via AI-driven industries may be focused in the fingers of some companies and people, further deepening economic inequality.

Furthermore, AI's potential to disproportionately affect low-income groups underscores the want for policymakers to take a proactive method in addressing the social and economic affects of these technology. This includes developing regulations that promote people' rights, ensure truthful distribution of wealth, and guide training and education packages to assist people adapt to the converting body of workers. Without such safeguards, AI's integration into the financial system may want to exacerbate current social divides and undermine efforts to promote monetary and social justice.

AI's position in social mobility and access to resources is some other vital vicinity where human rights and social order intersect. AI has the ability to beautify social mobility by using improving get admission to to training, healthcare, and other offerings, specifically in remote or underserved areas. For instance, AI-powered academic systems can offer personalised learning experiences for college students, and AI-pushed healthcare systems can improve analysis and remedy plans. These improvements have the ability to democratize get right of entry to to critical services and make contributions to social fairness.

However, the digital divide remains a good sized obstacle to the great blessings of AI. Individuals in low-earnings groups or rural areas may lack get admission to to the technology and infrastructure needed to gain from AI-pushed services. As AI will become greater included into various sectors, those with out get admission to to the internet, digital gadgets, or AI-enabled structures may be left at the back of, exacerbating present inequalities in schooling, healthcare, and employment.

To ensure that AI promotes social order and human rights, it is vital to deal with the virtual divide and ensure equitable access to AI-driven services. This consists of making sure that marginalized groups have get admission to to the equipment and resources essential to participate inside the virtual economy and society. By doing so, AI can grow to be a effective tool for advancing human rights and promoting social justice, as opposed to reinforcing current electricity structures and inequalities.

AI's effect on social order and human rights is multifaceted and calls for cautious consideration as those technologies maintain to adapt. While AI has the capability to beautify governance, enhance security, and promote social mobility, it additionally raises full-size concerns related to privacy, discrimination, monetary inequality, and access to assets. As AI keeps to shape the future of society, it is vital to expand moral and legal frameworks that make certain those technology are deployed in approaches that defend and sell human rights for all. By addressing these challenges proactively, we will create a future where AI contributes to a simply, equitable, and rights-respecting society.

6.3. Rights and Ethical Concerns

As artificial intelligence (AI) maintains to permeate all aspects of human existence, the rights and ethical worries surrounding its use are developing extra complex and urgent. The integration of AI into areas such as healthcare, justice, education, employment, or even warfare brings both first rate opportunities and large risks. These traits task existing moral frameworks and human rights requirements, posing crucial questions about the balance among technological development and the safeguarding of man or woman freedoms and dignity.

AI has the potential to strengthen human rights by enhancing get entry to to vital services, decreasing poverty, and promoting fairness in many fields. However, it additionally risks undermining the very rights it guarantees to uphold, elevating vital ethical dilemmas. The anxiety among AI's capacity for tremendous social impact and its capability to infringe upon man or woman rights is central to ongoing debates about how society should modify and govern AI technologies.

One of the maximum instant and extensively mentioned moral worries related to AI is the issue of privacy. AI systems, specifically those employed in surveillance, records mining, and social media, have the capability to gather and analyze sizeable amounts of personal records. This facts can variety from seemingly harmless statistics, which include online purchasing habits or surfing history, to greater sensitive information, which includes clinical facts, private communications, or even facial reputation facts.

The great collection of private data via AI systems increases tremendous privateness issues. While such structures can be used to customise offerings and enhance efficiency, additionally they open the door to mass surveillance and manipulate. For example, AI-powered facial reputation technology can music individuals in public areas without their consent, doubtlessly violating their privateness rights. Additionally, the use of AI in predictive policing or countrywide security should result in the profiling and concentrated on of people primarily based on private statistics, doubtlessly infringing upon their civil liberties.

These issues spotlight the need for robust moral pointers and felony frameworks to shield privateness in an AI-driven international. While AI has the capacity to improve lives in numerous approaches, its potential to collect and examine personal facts needs that human rights be positioned at the forefront of discussions regarding the improvement and deployment of AI technologies.

Another significant moral difficulty associated with AI is the danger of algorithmic bias and discrimination. AI systems are designed to analyze from statistics, however the best of the records used to train those structures is important in determining how well they feature. If AI algorithms are trained on biased or incomplete datasets, they can perpetuate or even exacerbate current inequalities.

For example, AI systems used in hiring practices, law enforcement, or mortgage approval processes can toughen existing biases based totally on race, gender, socioeconomic popularity, or incapacity. Studies have shown that AI-driven hiring platforms might also desire male candidates over lady candidates or white candidates over minority candidates if the underlying records displays such biases. Similarly, predictive policing algorithms can disproportionately goal sure racial or ethnic corporations, main to unfair remedy and deepening social divides.

The moral problem right here is that AI structures, while now not cautiously monitored and examined for equity, can also inadvertently violate the principles of equality and non-discrimination. As AI will become greater incorporated into essential choice-making approaches, it's far critical to ensure that the data used to educate these systems is numerous, inclusive, and consultant of all groups. Additionally, ongoing audits and accountability mechanisms are critical to identifying and addressing biases that can end up AI structures evolve.

AI structures, mainly those driven by using system getting to know and deep mastering algorithms, have the ability to make choices autonomously, regularly with out human intervention or oversight. While this could lead to efficiencies and pace, it also raises enormous ethical worries approximately accountability and manipulate.

When an AI system makes a selection that harms an person or a group, it could be difficult to determine who's responsible. Is it the developer who created the algorithm? The company that deployed the AI machine? Or the AI itself, which is acting primarily based on styles discovered from facts? The question of duty becomes even more urgent in high-stakes scenarios, which includes independent vehicles, clinical AI structures, or navy drones, wherein the effects of failure can be intense.

This problem of control and obligation is carefully tied to human rights, as people have to be able to accept as true with that the systems governing their lives are transparent, accountable, and designed to shield their nicely-being. Ethical frameworks surrounding AI need to deal with these worries through establishing clear suggestions for liability and oversight. Furthermore, there should be mechanisms to ensure that AI systems remain situation to human manage, especially whilst they may be utilized in excessive-hazard environments or regions affecting fundamental rights.

AI's developing role within the financial system increases critical questions about the future of labor, monetary rights, and the capacity for enormous activity displacement. AI has the potential to automate a huge variety of responsibilities, from guide labor to cognitive features together with customer support, legal evaluation, or even innovative paintings. While this can cause accelerated productivity and efficiency, it additionally poses a risk to people in many industries.

The moral difficulty right here is that AI ought to result in massive unemployment and financial inequality, in particular for people in low-skilled jobs or industries prone to automation. If AI is capable of update human employees, many may additionally discover themselves out of work with out the abilities needed for brand spanking new jobs created by means of AI technology. This could exacerbate current social and monetary inequalities, undermining the right to paintings and the proper to an ok wellknown of dwelling.

To cope with those issues, there need to be a focal point on growing a simply transition for employees displaced through AI. This consists of investing in schooling and retraining programs, growing social protection nets, and making sure that the blessings of AI-pushed productiveness profits are shared greater equitably across society. Failure to deal with those troubles should result in an AI-pushed economic system that disproportionately advantages a small elite, whilst leaving huge segments of the population behind.

As AI technology hold to conform, there may be a developing challenge approximately who gets to determine how AI is evolved and used. The moral problem here relates to the right of individuals and groups to have a voice in shaping the future of AI. Given that AI is in all likelihood to have profound consequences on surely every aspect of society, it's miles essential that numerous views are covered within the choice-making method.

This consists of making sure that marginalized groups, whose interests are frequently ignored, have a say in how AI is used and controlled. It additionally involves promoting transparency and openness in AI development, so that the general public can understand how AI structures are being created, examined, and deployed. By ensuring that AI development is participatory and inclusive, we are able to assist make sure that AI technology serve the broader public top, in place of the interests of a pick few.

The ethical concerns surrounding AI and its effect on human rights are good sized and complicated. From privateness and surveillance to algorithmic bias, autonomy, and financial displacement, AI offers both remarkable possibilities and extreme dangers. As AI continues to adapt, it's far essential that policymakers, builders, and society as a whole engage in considerate discussions approximately how to make sure that AI is used in ways that uphold human rights and ethical standards.

This requires no longer handiest the development of strong prison and regulatory frameworks but additionally a dedication to ongoing speak and ethical reflection. Only via a careful and inclusive method can we make sure that AI contributes definitely to society and respects the rights and dignity of individuals.

CHAPTER 7

AI and Creative People

7.1. Creative Thinking and AI

The dating between innovative questioning and synthetic intelligence (AI) offers one of the maximum compelling and complicated discussions in the discipline of ethics, generation, and the destiny of human intellect. Traditionally, creativity has been considered one of the uniquely human developments, a manifestation of recognition, self-expression, and emotional intensity. However, the increasing abilties of AI are starting to task this conventional view, main to a re-evaluation of what creativity really way in an generation of intelligent machines.

At its core, creativity is regularly visible because the ability to provide authentic ideas, solutions, or inventive expressions which can be novel and precious. For humans, creativity isn't simply a made from intelligence or expertise however a deeply intuitive and emotional process intertwined with cultural, social, and private affects. It draws from a sizable array of reviews, emotions, or even unconscious thoughts, shaping how individuals technique challenges and possibilities.

Creative thinking isn't always confined to the arts but extends to technological know-how, trouble-solving, and the technology of latest standards. It entails divergent questioning, the ability to look connections among reputedly unrelated ideas, and the ability to transcend traditional limitations. Human creativity is inherently tied to our emotional and mental states, our reviews, and our inherent preference to discover the unknown.

Artificial intelligence, alternatively, operates essentially differently from human cognition. AI systems, in particular those driven by way of device studying, are designed to research big amounts of information, apprehend styles, and make predictions primarily based on that records. While this capability lets in AI to mimic certain aspects of human intelligence, it does no longer possess the intrinsic emotional or experiential elements that fuel human creativity.

Yet, AI's role in creativity is plain. By processing and studying extensive datasets a long way past the capability of a human mind, AI can generate innovative ideas, answers, and inventive expressions that may not be right away obvious to human thinkers. AI is already being used to create tune, literature, visual arts, or even architectural designs. Tools which includes generative antagonistic networks (GANs) permit for the advent of practical snap shots, motion pictures, and artistic endeavors that seem like created by means of humans, but are produced via machines. These algorithms can remix current content material, create versions, and even generate entirely new works primarily based on existing styles, genres, and styles.

One distinguished instance is using AI in tune composition. AI systems like OpenAI's MuseNet and Jukedeck can compose song in diverse genres by way of reading present musical works and the use of gadget getting to know techniques to generate new compositions that mimic the structures and types of classical, jazz, electronic, and even cutting-edge pop song. Similarly, within the visual arts, AI-generated paintings and drawings had been sold at public sale for widespread sums, showcasing the industrial ability of AI in inventive creation.

Rather than viewing AI as a replacement for human creativity, it is able to be more productive to view it as a device that could beautify and collaborate with human creativity. AI can help inside the creative technique by means of imparting new thoughts, automating repetitive tasks, and allowing quicker prototyping and experimentation. For instance, image designers and illustrators can use AI to generate tough sketches or concepts, which they could then refine and customize. Writers can appoint AI to generate plot thoughts or assist with language patterns, as a result accelerating the writing manner and presenting a fresh angle.

In this collaborative model, AI serves as a creative partner as opposed to a rival. The integration of AI into the innovative method demanding situations traditional notions of authorship and originality. When a system assists in creating a work of art, who owns the highbrow belongings? Is it the human who directed the AI, or the device that performed the assignment? These questions delve into complex ethical and legal territory, raising essential troubles approximately the nature of creativity itself.

AI has the potential to democratize creativity through enabling folks that won't have the identical degree of talent or education to engage in artistic endeavors. Through user-friendly equipment and platforms, everyone can create visible artwork, tune, or written works, even without conventional inventive education. This opens up creative fields to a broader variety of humans and fosters a greater inclusive know-how of what creativity can be.

As AI maintains to evolve, ethical issues surrounding its role in creative techniques intensify. One of the primary issues is the ability for AI to supply works that may be indistinguishable from human-created content material. While this has the capability to revolutionize the humanities, it also increases questions about the authenticity of AI-generated works. If a device can create artwork, song, or literature that rivals the work of human artists, what does this suggest for the cost of human creativity?

Another large moral problem is the potential for AI to perpetuate biases gift in the information it's miles trained on. If AI is used to generate creative works primarily based on ancient information this is biased or incomplete, there is a hazard that AI-generated content material ought to improve stereotypes or fail to represent various voices and perspectives.

This should restriction the scope of creativity and make contributions to a homogenization of inventive output.

Additionally, the upward push of AI-generated content material increases questions about highbrow belongings rights. As machines start to produce innovative works, figuring out who owns the rights to those works becomes more and more complex. Should the author of the AI gadget be considered the proprietor, or is it the man or woman who makes use of the AI to generate the paintings? These criminal and moral concerns will in all likelihood form the future of AI in creative industries.

Looking ahead, the position of AI in creativity will probably keep to adapt. AI will no longer update human creativity, but it will increase and rework how we reflect onconsideration on and have interaction with the innovative procedure. Artists, musicians, writers, and other creatives will probable continue to collaborate with AI, the usage of its computational energy to push the limits in their paintings.

However, as AI becomes extra included into creative fields, there will be a want for greater reflection on the moral, philosophical, and felony implications of this partnership. Questions surrounding authorship, ownership, and the authenticity of AI-generated content material will require ongoing discussion and backbone. The relationship between human creativity and AI is not one among competition, however of cooperation, and it's going to take careful navigation to make sure that this collaboration stays ethically sound and artistically enriching.

In end, the intersection of innovative questioning and AI represents a profound shift in how we recognize and interact with art, innovation, and human potential. While AI may additionally by no means fully reflect the nuanced, emotional depth of human creativity, its ability to supplement and decorate human creative expression offers thrilling new possibilities for the destiny of creativity. Whether through collaborative partnerships or as a tool for character expression, AI is poised to redefine the boundaries of what we will create and imagine. The key could be ensuring that this variation happens in a way that respects the moral, cultural, and emotional dimensions of creativity, and that it serves to increase, as opposed to lessen, the unique human spirit that lies at the heart of all creative undertaking.

7.2. Machine Creativity and Ethical Values

The concept of gadget creativity is at the forefront of discussions surrounding artificial intelligence (AI) and its effect on the arts, generation, and society. As AI systems become an increasing number of sophisticated, they may be capable of generating works that can be categorised as innovative, consisting of art work, song, poetry, and even structure. However, as machines display the ability to create, they project our traditional notions of creativity, originality, and artistic expression. This transformation raises critical questions on the intersection of system creativity and ethical values.

Machine creativity refers back to the potential of AI structures to generate outputs which can be commonly related to human creativity. These systems, frequently primarily based on algorithms like deep getting to know and generative opposed networks (GANs), analyze big datasets to perceive styles and systems, which they then use to provide new and regularly progressive content. The scope of gadget creativity is enormous: AI can compose track, write stories, paint, layout merchandise, or even generate new clinical hypotheses. In many instances, the works produced by way of those machines are indistinguishable from those created by means of human artists, blurring the traces between what we historically view as human-created and device-generated content.

Despite these capabilities, device creativity lacks the intrinsic human characteristics that underpin the creative system. AI does no longer own feelings, recognition, or the lived reviews that gasoline human artistic expression. Instead, it relies on mathematical models, facts-pushed procedures, and predefined rules to provide innovative works. Therefore, the query arises: Can system-generated works simply be taken into consideration creative, or are they certainly the result of complex algorithms manipulating statistics in a way that mimics creativity?

While AI systems can generate new combinations of existing styles, they do now not have the emotional or subjective experiences that tell the creativity of human beings. As a result, some argue that device creativity isn't "proper" creativity, but alternatively a simulation of creativity. The ethical implications of this distinction are extensive, as they challenge our information of what constitutes unique idea and artistic price.

The emergence of machine creativity brings with it more than a few ethical issues, particularly with regards to authorship, originality, and the ability effect on human artists and cultural expression. One of the central moral problems is the question of authorship: Who owns a piece created via AI? If a system generates a piece of artwork or music, is the creator the programmer who advanced the AI, the person who directed the gadget, or the machine itself?

This predicament is complicated by way of the reality that AI does no longer have the equal rights or fame as human creators. For example, if a portray created by means of an AI is offered at an public sale, who ought to get hold of the earnings? The developer of the AI? The proprietor of the system? Or does the AI itself deserve recognition? As AI structures become more independent, these questions turns into more and more complicated and could require prison frameworks to deal with possession and intellectual assets rights.

Another ethical challenge revolves across the capacity for AI to perpetuate biases present inside the records it's miles skilled on. AI algorithms are most effective as true as the facts they may be fed, and if that records is biased or incomplete, the device-generated output might also replicate those biases. For instance, an AI skilled on a dataset of artworks created predominantly via male artists can also produce work that reflects gendered biases, probably reinforcing stereotypes or proscribing the diversity of artistic expression.

Moreover, there may be the threat that gadget creativity should dilute or update human creativity, especially in industries in which originality and artistry are fairly valued. As AI-generated works become more familiar, there is a concern that human artists could warfare to compete, particularly if AI is used to produce massive quantities of artwork fast and at lower cost. This should cause economic and cultural shifts within the artwork world, where human creators may find themselves displaced by means of machines which can reflect or maybe surpass their paintings in certain approaches.

As machines tackle more innovative roles, it's miles essential to ensure that moral values are embedded inside the design and use of AI structures. One of the key values in this context is the protection of human dignity and the recognition of the intrinsic well worth of human creativity. While AI can increase and assist within the innovative process, it's far vital to recollect that human creativity is not pretty much producing aesthetically captivating outcomes or fixing issues. It is about expressing ideas, feelings, and reports that mirror our shared humanity.

Incorporating ethical values into the development of AI is important to ensuring that AI-pushed creativity serves to enhance human culture in preference to undermine it. This consists of prioritizing transparency, fairness, and accountability within the layout of AI systems. Developers have to make sure that the algorithms underlying AI creativity are unfastened from biases and are able to generate numerous and inclusive outputs. Additionally, AI systems ought to be designed with an consciousness of their ability social and cultural effect, and their use must be guided by using ideas that promote ethical and accountable engagement with era.

Furthermore, ethical values associated with the authenticity and originality of innovative works should be addressed. While AI can produce works that mimic the sorts of well-known artists or invent new genres, it is important to consider the function of human enter inside the creative system. AI need to no longer be visible alternatively for human creativity, but as a tool that complements and complements it. For example, artists may also use AI to experiment with new forms or ideas, but the very last work need to still mirror the human experience, rationale, and emotional connection that is imperative to true creativity.

As AI keeps to evolve, the future of system creativity will probable be formed by way of ongoing advancements in AI technology, in addition to via the ethical frameworks we establish for its use. One potential destiny improvement is the increased integration of AI into collaborative innovative tactics. Rather than changing human artists, AI should come to be a treasured creative accomplice, helping artists explore new ideas, enlarge their inventive horizons, and push the limits of traditional media.

In the music enterprise, for instance, AI could help composers generate novel sounds or harmonies, which human musicians ought to then construct upon and refine. In visible arts, AI may want to offer new gear for experimentation, enabling artists to create works that have been formerly not possible. Such collaborations between human beings and machines should cause interesting innovations in art and lifestyle.

At the equal time, as AI turns into more capable of generating works which are indistinguishable from those created by using humans, we are able to want to rethink the position of human creativity in artistic expression. Will the fee of artwork shift from the artist's identification and emotional connection to the work, to the output itself, irrespective of its foundation? And if so, how do we determine the really worth of a work of artwork in a global in which machines are able to growing at an unparalleled scale?

The ethical challenges of gadget creativity aren't easily resolved. As AI structures keep to develop and combine into creative industries, it will be vital for society to interact in ongoing conversations approximately the position of machines within the inventive technique, the ownership and value of AI-generated works, and the effect of AI on human way of life. By ensuring that ethical concepts are upheld and that AI is used responsibly, we are able to ensure that system creativity serves as a device for increasing the bounds of human inventive expression, in preference to diminishing its significance.

In end, the intersection of gadget creativity and moral values represents a complicated and evolving task. As AI systems benefit the capacity to create, they push the boundaries of what we recognize as creativity, wondering the traditional differences among human and device-generated art. By embedding moral ideas into the development and application of AI, we are able to manual the evolution of system creativity in a manner that respects human dignity, promotes inclusivity, and fosters a rich and various cultural landscape. The future of creativity, both human and gadget-driven, could be fashioned through the values we uphold and the selections we make within the age of AI.

7.3. AI and Human Intelligence

The courting between synthetic intelligence (AI) and human intelligence is one of the most profound and debated subjects within the realms of technology, philosophy, and ethics. As AI systems retain to conform and reap extraordinary feats in obligations historically taken into consideration distinct to human cognition—consisting of getting to know, choice-making, and innovative endeavors—questions rise up about the character of intelligence itself. Can AI possess intelligence equivalent to human intelligence? What does it suggest for something to be "sensible," and the way does human intelligence examine to the capabilities of machines?

Human intelligence is complicated, multifaceted, and formed by way of a combination of genetic factors, environmental affects, and person reports. Traditionally, human intelligence has been measured via cognitive abilties inclusive of reasoning, hassle-fixing, abstract thinking, reminiscence, and gaining knowledge of. However, those talents aren't restrained to aware concept or good judgment. Human intelligence also encompasses emotional intelligence—the ability to apprehend and control one's very own feelings and apprehend feelings in others—in addition to social intelligence, which includes navigating relationships, empathy, and conversation.

Unlike AI, human intelligence is deeply intertwined with focus and subjective revel in. Humans are not merely hassle-solvers; they possess awareness, self-reflection, and feelings that manual their decision-making methods. Cognitive neuroscientists and philosophers have long debated the nature of attention and whether machines could ever revel in it in a comparable way to humans. At the core of these debates is the query: Can AI be sincerely clever if it lacks subjective experience or attention?

Artificial intelligence, however, is described with the aid of machines which can be designed to perform duties that might normally require human intelligence. AI systems can be categorized into slender AI (also referred to as susceptible AI) and wellknown AI (additionally called sturdy AI). Narrow AI refers to systems which can be designed for precise obligations, inclusive of facial recognition, language translation, or independent riding. These structures excel at appearing the duties they're programmed for but lack the ability to generalize their intelligence to different contexts or responsibilities. General AI, which stays in large part theoretical at this level, refers to AI that could carry out any intellectual mission that a human can do, showing reasoning, creativity, and mastering in a way that mirrors human talents.

The purpose of AI studies is to create machines that can think, examine, and adapt like human beings. However, modern AI technology nevertheless fall quick of replicating the full spectrum of human intelligence. Despite their capability to method great amounts of statistics and solve issues in especially specialised domains, AI systems nevertheless lack the depth of know-how, instinct, and emotional intelligence that human beings deliver to many elements of life.

While AI has made outstanding strides in mimicking certain factors of human intelligence, there are several key variations between the two that spotlight the restrictions of machines:

1. Consciousness and Self-Awareness: One of the defining capabilities of human intelligence is awareness—the attention of 1's personal lifestyles, mind, and feelings. Human beings aren't handiest aware about the arena around them but additionally have the potential for introspection. In evaluation, AI systems perform based totally on pre-programmed guidelines and learned statistics styles with out cognizance. While AI can simulate behaviors that seem sensible, it lacks subjective experience and self-cognizance. This increases questions about whether AI ought to ever achieve genuine recognition, or if it'll continually be restrained to processing facts with out true expertise.

2. Emotions and Empathy: Emotional intelligence is an important aspect of human cognition. Humans are able to recognize feelings in themselves and others, and their emotional responses often manual decision-making and

interpersonal interactions. AI structures, but, do no longer have emotions. While AI may be programmed to understand and respond to emotional cues (for example, thru sentiment evaluation in textual content or facial popularity software program), these responses are based on algorithms as opposed to genuine feelings. This loss of emotional intensity limits AI's capacity to engage in in reality empathetic interactions and makes it unlikely that AI will ever absolutely mirror the emotional richness of human intelligence.

3. Creativity and Intuition: While AI systems can generate innovative outputs—which include composing track, writing poetry, or designing new merchandise—these outputs are based totally on styles and facts that the machine has been educated on. Human creativity, however, involves intuition, originality, and the ability to suppose "outside the box." Human intelligence isn't always constrained by statistics; it attracts on creativeness, inspiration, and experience to create something totally new. In assessment, AI's creativity is confined via its programming and statistics, which means it can't produce without a doubt authentic ideas within the identical manner that humans can.

4. Flexibility and Adaptability: Human intelligence is exceptionally adaptable. Humans can learn a extensive form of obligations, follow expertise across one-of-a-kind domain names, and fast regulate to new and unpredictable situations. AI systems, however, are generally designed for specific tasks

and can war when confronted with unusual scenarios. While machine getting to know algorithms allow AI to improve its performance over the years, it's far nonetheless a long way more rigid than human intelligence in its capability to transfer expertise from one context to every other.

5. Ethical Reasoning and Moral Judgment: Human intelligence is guided via ethical and moral reasoning. People make decisions based totally no longer handiest on logic and facts but additionally on values, standards, and a feel of proper and incorrect. AI, in comparison, is guided by using the parameters set by way of its creators and does no longer have the ability to make moral judgments on its personal. While AI can be programmed to comply with moral hints or make selections that align with certain moral ideas, it does now not "understand" the motives in the back of these decisions. This dilemma will become particularly essential whilst AI is utilized in situations that require moral discernment, which includes autonomous vehicles or healthcare.

As AI continues to evolve, the bounds between gadget intelligence and human intelligence may additionally blur in addition. Some futurists envision a international wherein AI will become so advanced that it may suit or maybe surpass human intelligence across all domain names, main to the development of artificial trendy intelligence (AGI). AGI would not most effective be able to remedy complex issues however additionally own the flexibility, creativity, and adaptive learning that signify human cognition.

While this prospect increases exciting possibilities, it also raises profound moral and existential questions. If AI surpasses human intelligence, what does this imply for the position of people in society? Will AI emerge as a device to beautify human capabilities, or could it lead to accidental consequences, including the displacement of humans from the workforce or even the lack of human autonomy? These questions underscore the significance of moral frameworks and responsible development in AI research.

The integration of AI into human life could also lead to a hybridization of human and gadget intelligence, where people enhance their cognitive abilties with AI-powered tools. Brain-pc interfaces (BCIs) and different neurotechnological advancements may want to allow people to work symbiotically with AI, augmenting their very own intelligence and increasing their cognitive capacities.

The ongoing development of AI forces us to reconsider the very nature of intelligence and the moral boundaries of technology. Is human intelligence precise, or is it merely a shape of complicated facts processing that can be replicated in machines? Can AI expand attention, or will it always be limited to mimicking sensible conduct? How ought to society navigate the challenges posed through increasingly more sophisticated

AI systems, specially in terms of privacy, autonomy, and equity?

One essential trouble is the capacity for AI to exacerbate inequalities. If AI systems turn out to be the primary drivers of innovation and choice-making, there may be a chance that certain companies—specifically those without get admission to to superior technology—will be left in the back of. It may be important to make certain that AI is developed and deployed in approaches that advantage society as an entire, rather than entrenching present strength structures.

In end, AI and human intelligence constitute two wonderful forms of cognition, every with its own strengths and boundaries. While AI may additionally at some point reap incredible feats of studying and hassle-fixing, it's miles not likely to ever completely replicate the richness and complexity of human intelligence. As AI continues to adapt, it will be essential to preserve a balance between technological progress and moral concerns, ensuring that the improvement of AI serves to enhance human existence as opposed to decrease it.

7.4. AI and the Future of Art and Innovation

Artificial intelligence is hastily remodeling the landscape of creativity and innovation, tough conventional notions of creative expression, authorship, and the very essence of human ingenuity. As AI systems end up capable of producing artwork, music, literature, design, or even medical hypotheses, society faces profound questions about the relationship among human creators and clever machines. The integration of AI into artistic and modern methods holds great promise for increasing creative opportunities, democratizing access to equipment, and accelerating breakthroughs. At the same time, it raises complex debates about originality, cultural value, ethics, and the destiny role of human creativeness.

One of the maximum placing impacts of AI on artwork is its ability to generate novel content autonomously or in collaboration with people. Generative models including GANs (Generative Adversarial Networks), transformer-primarily based language models, and neural style transfer algorithms permit the introduction of pics, texts, and sounds which could rival human-produced works in complexity and attraction. Artists increasingly more use AI as a innovative partner, leveraging algorithms to discover new patterns, remix present works, or transcend human technical limitations. This symbiosis opens unexplored aesthetic territories and redefines creative processes as iterative dialogues between human instinct and computational creativity.

AI-driven innovation extends beyond the humanities into scientific and technological realms. Machine mastering accelerates hypothesis era, optimizes design spaces, and automates experimentation. From drug discovery to materials science and engineering, AI structures find patterns and answers which could elude human cognition, enhancing problem-solving capacities. This fusion of human insight and AI's analytical power reconfigures innovation workflows, enabling greater rapid and various avenues of exploration.

However, the upward push of AI-generated artwork demanding situations traditional standards of authorship and intellectual belongings. If an art work is created primarily by an AI machine, who holds the copyright? The programmer, the consumer, or the gadget? Legal systems international grapple with those questions, searching for to balance incentives for innovation with recognition of innovative corporation. Furthermore, concerns stand up about the devaluation of human creativity and the ability commodification of artwork produced en masse by way of algorithms.

Cultural implications additionally merit interest. Art is deeply embedded in human enjoy, reflecting identity, records, and social critique. AI-generated content, whilst wonderful, may lack contextual intensity or emotional authenticity perceived in human creations. Yet, AI also can function a tool for cultural renovation, restoring lost works or allowing access to creative traditions via digital manner. The interaction between AI and cultural history opens possibilities for each innovation and maintenance.

Ethical issues accompany AI's role in artwork and innovation. The use of datasets containing copyrighted or culturally sensitive substances raises questions about consent and representation. Biases embedded in education facts can perpetuate stereotypes or marginalize voices. Transparent practices, inclusive datasets, and participatory methods can assist ensure AI fosters diverse and respectful creative ecosystems.

Accessibility is every other transformative element. AI-powered gear decrease boundaries for beginner creators via simplifying technical skills required for complicated creative production. This democratization can empower people from numerous backgrounds, enriching the cultural landscape with new perspectives. At the same time, it challenges gatekeeping establishments and reshapes creative economies.

Looking beforehand, the co-evolution of human creativity and AI guarantees a destiny wherein innovation is amplified with the aid of symbiotic partnerships. Augmented creativity, where AI complements human creativeness with out supplanting it, represents a compelling paradigm. Emphasizing human values, emotional resonance, and cultural context in AI design could be crucial to nurture this partnership.

AI is reshaping artwork and innovation in profound ways, providing unheard of opportunities and complicated challenges. By thoughtfully integrating AI into creative and medical domain names, society can harness its capacity to enlarge human expression, boost up discovery, and foster inclusive innovation. Navigating this future calls for balancing technological development with ethical stewardship, cultural sensitivity, and a reaffirmation of the irreplaceable characteristics of human creativeness.

CHAPTER 8

Ethics and AI: Future Challenges

8.1. The Future and Ethical Issues

As synthetic intelligence (AI) maintains to conform at an exponential rate, the ethical problems surrounding its improvement and integration into society are getting increasingly more pressing. The future of AI is full of promise, with ability advancements that would revolutionize healthcare, schooling, transportation, and truely each other thing of human lifestyles. However, these advancements include vast moral challenges that want to be addressed carefully to make certain that AI technologies are developed and deployed in ways that gain humanity without causing harm.

One of the vital moral worries related to AI is the question of autonomy—each for machines and for the folks who engage with them. As AI structures emerge as an increasing number of self sufficient, there may be a developing concern about how an awful lot decision-making energy need to be entrusted to those structures, in particular in excessive-stakes regions including healthcare, crook justice, and self sustaining automobiles.

For example, in the context of autonomous vehicles, AI systems are tasked with making break up-second choices that could have existence-or-demise results. Should an AI system in a self-riding automobile be programmed to prioritize the safety of the vehicle's passengers over the safety of pedestrians? What ethical principles have to manual these choices? And, perhaps most significantly, who need to be held chargeable for the actions of AI structures that make such decisions? These are complicated questions that venture conventional notions of duty and accountability.

Similarly, in healthcare, AI systems are being developed to assist in diagnosing illnesses, recommending remedies, or even performing surgical procedures. While these systems can extensively improve outcomes and reduce human mistakes, they also increase questions on autonomy. Should AI have the authority to make clinical choices without human intervention? And how do we ensure that sufferers' rights and dignity are upheld when AI is concerned in their care?

The developing autonomy of AI systems raises essential questions about the nature of human selection-making and whether or not AI can ever mirror the nuanced, fee-based totally choices that humans make. While AI may additionally excel at processing facts and making goal decisions based totally on algorithms, it lacks the human ability to remember context, feelings, and ethical issues. This raises the difficulty of whether or not machines must ever take delivery of the electricity to make choices that basically have an effect on people's lives.

Another urgent moral problem with AI inside the destiny is the query of privateness. As AI systems become extra integrated into ordinary life, they may have get admission to to substantial amounts of personal information, which includes touchy statistics which include medical facts, financial information, and social behaviors. While this facts can be used to improve offerings and beautify decision-making, it also presents large dangers in terms of privacy and surveillance.

The potential of AI structures to process and analyze big datasets enables organizations, governments, and different corporations to display people on an exceptional scale. Facial popularity technology, for instance, has the ability for use for mass surveillance, elevating concerns approximately individuals' proper to privacy and freedom from unwarranted government or company intrusion. The series and analysis of private facts through AI structures can also cause discrimination, as algorithms may additionally inadvertently perpetuate biases gift inside the records.

As AI technologies preserve to develop, there may be an increasing need for robust rules and frameworks that defend people' privacy and save you the abuse of AI in surveillance. Striking the proper balance among utilising AI to enhance services and protecting individuals' rights will be a key moral assignment within the coming years.

The speedy development of AI technology additionally increases concerns approximately inequality and the displacement of human employees. AI and automation have the potential to revolutionize industries by way of growing performance, lowering expenses, and allowing new abilties. However, this comes with the threat of good sized job displacement, especially in sectors that rely upon ordinary and guide exertions.

As AI structures emerge as greater capable, there may be a actual challenge that many jobs, specifically the ones in production, transportation, and customer service, will get replaced through machines. While new jobs may additionally emerge as a end result of AI improvements, there is no guarantee that displaced people could be able to transition into these new roles, specifically if they lack the necessary abilities. This ought to exacerbate current social and monetary inequalities, as the advantages of AI can also accrue disproportionately to those with the competencies and resources to take advantage of the new possibilities, even as those without such benefits can be left in the back of.

Moreover, AI has the capability to further entrench inequalities by exacerbating the wealth gap. Companies that manage AI technologies ought to gather enormous quantities of wealth, while individuals and groups that are already marginalized may want to face in addition economic difficulty. The unequal distribution of AI's advantages and the ability for job displacement boost critical ethical questions about fairness and justice in an increasingly more automated international.

To cope with those worries, policymakers will need to remember approaches to ensure that the benefits of AI are distributed equitably and that employees are supported via transitions to new styles of employment. This could include investing in education and education packages that equip people with the abilties wanted in an AI-driven economic system, in addition to exploring answers which include familiar primary income to mitigate the results of process displacement.

As AI systems turn out to be greater self sufficient and included into numerous factors of society, the problem of accountability turns into increasingly complex. Who is responsible whilst an AI device causes harm, makes an unethical decision, or fails to perform as predicted? Is it the developer who created the device, the business enterprise that deployed it, or the consumer who relied on it? The conventional legal and moral frameworks for duty are not properly-ready to handle the challenges posed by means of AI.

For instance, within the case of a self-riding car that reasons an coincidence, have to the manufacturer of the car be held accountable, or should the AI gadget be treated as an self reliant agent with criminal rights and duties? Similarly, if an AI device in healthcare makes a misdiagnosis that results in a affected person's dying, who need to be held dependable—the builders, the healthcare issuer, or the AI gadget itself?

The trouble of accountability is particularly complicated within the context of AI systems that analyze and adapt over time. If an AI machine evolves in unpredictable approaches, it is able to emerge as difficult to decide who is accountable for its moves. This underscores the want for new criminal frameworks which can cope with the specific challenges of AI and make sure that individuals and companies are held responsible for the results of AI structures.

As AI technology continue to shape the future, the function of ethics of their development and deployment becomes increasingly vital. Ethical issues ought to be incorporated into every stage of AI improvement, from layout to implementation, to make certain that AI systems are advanced in ways that align with societal values and human rights.

Researchers, developers, and policymakers need to work together to establish ethical pointers for AI improvement that prioritize transparency, fairness, and accountability. This consists of ensuring that AI systems are designed to be explainable, so that their choices can be understood and scrutinized via human beings. It additionally way considering the capacity social, monetary, and environmental impacts of AI technology and making sure that they are deployed in approaches that sell the general public correct.

In the destiny, AI has the ability to result in transformative modifications in society. However, realizing its full potential will require careful interest to the moral problems that get up as those technology evolve. By addressing issues related to autonomy, privateness, inequality, and accountability, we will ensure that AI is developed and deployed in methods that gain humanity and help construct a more just and equitable future.

8.2. Artificial Intelligence, Humanity, and the Ethical Future

The destiny of synthetic intelligence (AI) guarantees transformative adjustments for humanity. From enhancing human abilties to addressing complicated worldwide demanding situations, AI has the capacity to reshape societies, economies, and cultures in ways that we've but to absolutely realise. However, these advancements also increase profound ethical questions about the relationship among AI and humanity. As AI continues to conform and come to be greater incorporated into daily lifestyles, it will more and more assignment our conventional notions of identity, agency, and morality.

At the heart of the ethical questions surrounding AI is the issue of human organisation—the ability of individuals to make selections and act in keeping with their will. As AI structures become extra autonomous and capable of making choices, one of the principal issues is the quantity to which they'll affect or maybe replace human selection-making.

In many areas of existence, AI is already beginning to take on roles historically held via people. For example, AI-powered systems are used to assist in medical diagnoses, make hiring decisions, and decide creditworthiness. While these structures can frequently outperform human beings in terms of performance and accuracy, additionally they improve questions on whether individuals will lose their capacity to make meaningful choices about their personal lives. If AI systems are making choices on behalf of people—decisions that have an effect on their careers, fitness, and well-being—in which does human agency give up and machine control begin?

Moreover, the potential for AI to surpass human intelligence increases even more profound moral issues. If AI systems become more clever than humans, they could theoretically make decisions and form the future in ways that human beings cannot absolutely apprehend or manage. This raises questions on how lots power need to be entrusted to machines, and whether or not human beings will hold the ability to form their very own destinies in a world increasingly ruled by means of AI.

As we flow forward, it will likely be crucial to ensure that AI structures are evolved in approaches that preserve human employer and autonomy. Ethical frameworks need to be set up to make sure that AI remains a tool that serves human hobbies, as opposed to one that replaces or overrides them.

One of the maximum sizeable ways in which AI will form the future of humanity is through its impact at the body of workers. AI and automation have the capability to revolutionize industries, growth productiveness, and reduce charges. However, those advancements also pose a extreme risk to jobs, particularly those that contain ordinary or guide hard work.

In industries which includes manufacturing, transportation, and customer service, AI is already getting used to automate responsibilities that have been once performed by way of people. While this could lead to extra efficiency, it additionally increases the ethical problem of job displacement. As AI systems turn out to be extra capable, they'll render massive segments of the group of workers obsolete, leaving many workers with out meaningful employment.

This potential disruption of the exertions market raises sizeable moral questions about how society should deal with the displacement of workers. Should we embrace normal primary earnings (UBI) as a method to provide financial help to the ones whose jobs are displaced by using AI? How are we able to ensure that the blessings of AI and automation are shared equitably throughout society, instead of concentrating wealth and electricity within the arms of a few businesses and people?

Furthermore, as AI systems take over extra responsibilities, there may be a growing need for workers to conform and gather new abilities. However, not all employees will have get right of entry to to the training and assets needed to transition into new roles. This raises issues approximately social inequality and the capability for AI to exacerbate present economic divides. The ethical duty of governments, corporations, and educational institutions can be critical in addressing these challenges and making sure that AI's blessings are broadly dispensed.

While AI's capacity for activity displacement is a chief concern, it also holds the promise of enhancing human talents in methods that have been as soon as thought impossible. AI structures can assist in clinical research, improve education, and offer insights into complicated troubles which include weather exchange and poverty. In many instances, AI can increase human intelligence, permitting people to solve troubles and make decisions that would be difficult or not possible for people on my own.

For example, inside the discipline of medicine, AI is being used to analyze tremendous quantities of clinical records and discover patterns that may be missed by using human doctors. This may want to lead to earlier diagnoses, greater powerful treatments, and in the long run shop limitless lives. Similarly, AI is getting used to broaden personalized studying systems which could tailor educational experiences to the man or woman desires of students, probably enhancing get entry to to exquisite education for humans around the arena.

In the destiny, the mixing of AI into human decision-making ought to cause a brand new technology of human flourishing, in which people are empowered to make greater informed and powerful choices in all regions of lifestyles. However, this capacity is contingent upon the ethical improvement and deployment of AI technologies.

Ethical concerns must ensure that AI structures are designed to enhance human capacity, rather than undermine it. This includes ensuring that AI systems are on hand, transparent, and fair, and they do no longer perpetuate existing biases or inequalities. It also method making sure that AI is utilized in approaches that promote human nicely-being, as opposed to for exploitative or dangerous purposes.

As AI keeps to enhance, there also are lengthy-term ethical risks that ought to be carefully considered. One of the maximum extensive issues is the opportunity of AI surpassing human intelligence, a situation frequently referred to as the "singularity." If AI systems have been to come to be massively extra intelligent than human beings, they could doubtlessly develop their very own dreams and agendas, which may not align with human values or pursuits. This could result in catastrophic results, mainly if AI systems are able to perform with more efficiency and pace than human decision-makers.

The prospect of AI structures performing independently of human manage raises the ethical difficulty of AI's potential to pose a threat to humanity itself. If AI have been to end up self reliant and pursue goals which are incompatible with human survival, what steps will be taken to prevent it from causing damage? How can we make sure that AI stays aligned with human values, even because it will become more capable?

Furthermore, the deployment of AI in navy and security contexts increases considerable ethical worries. Autonomous guns structures, for instance, ought to potentially make lifestyles-or-death decisions without human intervention, raising questions on duty, proportionality, and the ethical use of force. The destiny improvement of AI in those regions will require careful oversight and worldwide cooperation to save you the misuse of AI technologies in conflict.

As AI continues to adapt, the moral demanding situations it provides would require ongoing mirrored image and debate. The future of AI will no longer be determined by using era by myself, however with the aid of the moral selections we make as a society. It is essential that we expand a sturdy ethical framework for AI that considers now not most effective the ability benefits of AI however also its risks and capacity harms.

Policymakers, builders, researchers, and ethicists ought to paintings together to make certain that AI is advanced and deployed in approaches that gain humanity as an entire. This includes setting up recommendations for the responsible improvement of AI, ensuring transparency and responsibility, and addressing the social, monetary, and political implications of AI technology.

The moral future of AI relies upon on our capacity to navigate those demanding situations and make decisions that align with our shared values. By making sure that AI is advanced in approaches that promote human properly-being, dignity, and justice, we will build a future in which AI complements, in place of diminishes, the human revel in.

8.3. The Long-Term Effects of AI on Society

As synthetic intelligence (AI) maintains to adapt at an unparalleled tempo, its lengthy-time period affects on society have become increasingly glaring. While AI holds great potential for improving diverse aspects of human lifestyles, from healthcare to training and transportation, it also raises profound questions on the societal shifts it may cause over the coming decades. These shifts will encompass changes within the group of workers, monetary structures, social dynamics, and even cultural norms.

One of the most profound changes AI is anticipated to carry is the transformation of the worldwide staff. As AI technologies enhance, many jobs which have historically been finished by means of people are possibly to be automatic. This fashion is already evident in industries which include production, transportation, and customer service, wherein AI-powered machines and robots are beginning to take over repetitive and manual obligations.

While AI has the potential to growth productivity and create new opportunities for innovation, it additionally poses good sized challenges to employment. The automation of routine jobs may want to result in substantial job displacement, especially for workers in low-skill and occasional-wage sectors. This shift ought to exacerbate social inequalities, as individuals with out the important talents or resources to transition into new roles can also find themselves excluded from the activity market.

Moreover, the character of work itself should trade. As AI takes over extra mundane and repetitive tasks, human people can be required to awareness on better-level obligations that call for creativity, trouble-solving, and emotional intelligence. This could result in a shift far from traditional forms of exertions and an elevated emphasis on jobs that require uniquely human abilities. However, this transition may be tough for workers to navigate without proper education and support.

To mitigate the potential poor consequences of AI on employment, it will likely be crucial to spend money on education and personnel development programs that help individuals adapt to new technologies and collect the capabilities needed for destiny jobs. Additionally, policymakers may also need to don't forget new financial models, including well-known simple profits (UBI), to make certain that individuals whose jobs are displaced via AI are nonetheless capable of maintain a respectable popular of dwelling.

AI is expected to have a profound impact on the worldwide financial system. As automation becomes extra large, sure industries might also see a dramatic reduction in hard work costs, main to extra performance and profitability. At the equal time, new industries and business models are probable to grow to be AI allows improvements that were as soon as idea impossible.

However, this economic disruption may cause good sized shifts in the distribution of wealth. Large companies which are able to leverage AI technology should gain a disproportionate amount of power and wealth, similarly consolidating their manage over markets. This may want to lead to more monetary inequality, as the benefits of AI are concentrated within the arms of some whilst many others are left at the back of.

The upward thrust of AI-pushed industries may also create new opportunities for wealth advent, but these possibilities might not be similarly accessible to all of us. Highly professional people in fields which include software program engineering, facts science, and AI development are likely to look improved call for for their services, at the same time as workers in extra recurring roles may also discover their abilities obsolete.

This redistribution of wealth and electricity could cause social unrest and heightened tensions among one of a kind socioeconomic businesses. It might be crucial for governments and global agencies to deal with these disparities by means of selling guidelines that make sure the truthful distribution of AI's benefits. Taxation reforms, social protection nets, and investments in education and schooling may be key to stopping the deepening of economic divides.

AI has the capacity to significantly regulate the social fabric of societies. As AI technology end up greater included into everyday life, they'll affect how people have interaction with one another, shape relationships, and participate in social and political lifestyles. The way wherein AI affects those social dynamics will rely largely on how it's far implemented and ruled.

One of the maximum pressing worries is the capacity for AI to exacerbate current social inequalities. If AI systems are developed and deployed in approaches that replicate the biases and prejudices in their creators, they could perpetuate or even intensify discrimination based on race, gender, socioeconomic fame, and different elements. For instance, AI algorithms utilized in hiring, lending, and regulation enforcement should unintentionally improve current disparities by means of favoring sure organizations over others.

Moreover, the significant use of AI ought to alter the manner people engage with each other within the public sphere. As AI structures take on extra roles traditionally stuffed by human beings—along with customer support representatives, fitness advisors, and even non-public companions—there may be a chance that human connections may want to become more transactional and less private. If AI starts offevolved to update human interplay in these areas, it may lead to social isolation and a decline in community engagement.

To deal with those problems, it is going to be critical to increase AI systems which might be obvious, responsible, and designed to promote social proper. Ethical frameworks and rules need to be established to make certain that AI technologies are used to reduce, rather than beef up, social inequalities. Additionally, efforts need to be made to make sure that AI does now not erode the social bonds which are vital for a healthy and thriving society.

In addition to the monetary and social influences of AI, its lengthy-term consequences will also be felt within the realm of subculture and psychology. As AI becomes greater capable of replicating human-like behaviors or even creating art, literature, and track, it can challenge traditional conceptions of creativity and identity.

For example, AI-generated works of art and literature enhance vital questions about authorship and originality. If a gadget can create a portray or write a singular that is indistinguishable from that of a human artist, who owns the rights to that paintings? What does it suggest for human creativity whilst machines can produce artwork that isn't best useful but also aesthetically attractive and emotionally resonant?

On a mental stage, the increasing presence of AI in every day existence ought to modify how individuals perceive themselves and their area in the world. If AI systems can outperform people in many regions, people may begin to question their very own skills and sense of motive. There is likewise the capacity for humans to end up overly reliant on AI, main to a diminished feel of employer and personal duty.

Furthermore, as AI will become extra advanced, it could trigger existential questions about the nature of attention and intelligence. If machines can showcase human-like traits, together with getting to know, adapting, and making decisions, it is able to assignment traditional notions of what it way to be human.

The cultural and psychological effect of AI would require cautious consideration as society movements forward. It could be critical to foster a dialogue approximately the role of AI in shaping human identification and creativity, whilst additionally making sure that people keep a sense of corporation and reason in a global increasingly inspired through machines.

The long-time period effects of AI on society will largely rely upon how AI technologies are governed. As AI systems come to be greater succesful and large, it is going to be crucial to set up clean moral guidelines and regulatory frameworks to make sure that their deployment is aligned with societal values and human rights.

Governments, global companies, and enterprise leaders have to paintings together to create regulations that promote the accountable improvement and use of AI. This includes making sure that AI is developed transparently, with enter from numerous stakeholders, and that its potential dangers are carefully evaluated and mitigated.

AI governance have to additionally prioritize the protection of human rights, making sure that AI does not infringe upon man or woman freedoms or contribute to the erosion of democracy. This may additionally contain the advent of recent legal guidelines and global agreements to modify AI's use in areas which includes surveillance, navy packages, and private facts series.

The long-term consequences of AI on society will depend on the choices we make today. By prioritizing ethical concerns and operating to make sure that AI is advanced for the advantage of all, we are able to create a destiny where AI complements, instead of undermines, the human revel in.

8.4. Global Governance of AI: International Cooperation

Artificial intelligence has emerged as a transformative force with international reach, transcending countrywide borders and influencing economies, societies, and safety landscapes global. The rapid development and deployment of AI technologies pose complicated challenges that no single usa can efficaciously cope with on my own. Issues along with ethical requirements, protection, privacy, responsibility, twin-use risks, and equitable get right of entry to require coordinated international governance. Global cooperation in AI governance is important to harmonize guidelines, prevent dangerous opposition, promote accountable innovation, and make certain that AI's blessings are shared inclusively and sustainably.

The transnational nature of AI development stems from the interconnectedness of digital infrastructure, the globalized float of data, and the international nature of era supply chains. AI research, talent, and capital are dispensed throughout continents, with collaboration and opposition unfolding concurrently among governments, agencies, and academia. This dynamic complicates unilateral regulatory strategies and highlights the need of multilateral frameworks that accommodate diverse hobbies and values while upholding essential standards.

A essential impetus for worldwide AI governance is the mitigation of risks associated with AI's dual-use capability.

Autonomous weapons, surveillance technology, and cyber competencies pose protection threats that would destabilize geopolitical balances or violate human rights. Without powerful cooperation, the threat of AI palms races or misuse escalates, with profound outcomes for global peace and balance. International treaties and agreements, analogous to those in nuclear non-proliferation or chemical weapons manage, are needed to establish norms, verification mechanisms, and accountability for AI programs with army or surveillance implications.

Ethical considerations underpin efforts to create shared frameworks for AI governance. Different cultures and felony systems convey various perspectives on privateness, equity, transparency, and human dignity. Inclusive international speak is required to perceive commonplace values and reconcile differences, making sure that AI governance displays pluralism instead of enforcing a unmarried worldview. Organizations along with the United Nations, UNESCO, the OECD, and specialised AI coalitions facilitate normative consensus-building thru pointers, concepts, and nice practices that tell national regulations and company conduct.

Data governance represents a essential component of international cooperation. Cross-border information flows gasoline AI systems however boost worries approximately sovereignty, security, and privateness. Establishing interoperable standards for facts protection, moral use, and equitable access can reduce fragmentation and enable accountable innovation. Agreements on statistics sharing, while respecting national policies, can accelerate medical discovery and cope with international challenges such as climate trade and public fitness crises.

Economic dimensions additionally motivate governance coordination. AI drives competitiveness in rising industries and hard work markets. Ensuring honest trade practices, stopping monopolistic dominance, and fostering ability-constructing in growing international locations are vital for equitable increase. International cooperation can sell technology transfer, schooling, and investment, lowering digital divides and enabling broader participation inside the AI-pushed financial system.

Implementation of world AI governance faces good sized limitations. Geopolitical rivalries, differing regulatory philosophies, and concerns over national sovereignty restrict consensus. Balancing protection with openness, innovation with precaution, and commercial pursuits with moral imperatives calls for diplomatic talent and mutual accept as true with. Mechanisms for enforcement, dispute decision, and tracking compliance continue to be underdeveloped.

Multi-stakeholder engagement is essential for effective governance. Governments, personal quarter actors, academia, civil society, and technical communities all contribute unique know-how and perspectives. Collaborative platforms allow shared problem-solving, transparency, and legitimacy. Initiatives inclusive of the Global Partnership on AI (GPAI) exemplify efforts to bridge sectors and countries in pursuit of accountable AI development.

Looking ahead, the established order of a robust international AI governance architecture will contain iterative methods of dialogue, norm-putting, capability-constructing, and adaptive regulation. It must stay flexible to accommodate technological advances and emerging demanding situations. Enhancing public cognizance and fostering international digital citizenship can empower people worldwide to participate in shaping AI's trajectory.

International cooperation is vital to control AI's transformative power responsibly and equitably. Through shared commitments, coordinated guidelines, and inclusive engagement, the worldwide community can harness AI's capability to deal with collective demanding situations, shield fundamental rights, and promote sustainable development. Navigating this complicated panorama demands visionary leadership, trust-building, and sustained collaboration to make sure that AI serves as a force for the not unusual true within the interconnected international.

www.ingramcontent.com/pod-product-compliance
Lightning Source LLC
LaVergne TN
LVHW051321050326
832903LV00031B/3297